Empty
Arms

Empty Arms

*Emotional Support For
Those Who Have Suffered a
Miscarriage, Stillbirth or
Tubal Pregnancy*

Pam Vredevelt

MULTNOMAH BOOKS
SISTERS, OREGON

Cover design by David Uttley
Cover Photography by Greg Shed

EMPTY ARMS: Emotional Support for Those Who Have Suffered Miscarriage or Stillbirth
©1984 by Multnomah Press Printed in the United States of America

LIBRARY OF CONGRESS CATALOGING IN PUBLICATION DATA

Vredevelt, Pam W., 1955-
  Empty arms.

  Bibliography: p.
    1. Miscarriage—Psychological aspects.   2. Stillbirth— Psychological aspects.   3. Bereavement—Psychological   aspects.
4. Chrishan life—1960–   I. Title.
RG648.V74   1984   155.9'37   84-2049
ISBN 0~8070-042-4 (pbk.)

94   95   96   97   98   99 - 15   14   13   12   11   10   9

Contents

Foreword

And God said, Let us make man in our image, after our likeness . . . So God created man in his own image, in the image of God created he him, male and female created he them. And God blessed them, and God said unto them, Be fruitful and multiply . . ." (Genesis 1:26-28 KJV).

Man . . . the crown of creation. Made in the image of God.

Through the miracle of conception God has actually given man the privilege of participating in the creation of life.

Although there will be no visible evidence for several months, a woman often knows she is pregnant within days. Even before the pregnancy is medically confirmed, she and her husband are praying, planning, and thanking God for their new baby.

But some times these hopes and aspirations are never realized due to the tragedy of miscarriage or stillbirth. Between 15% to 25% of all human conceptions do not successfully complete the twentieth week of pregnancy. More lives are lost in the first twenty weeks of pregnancy than are accumulatively lost in the next sixty-five years of life. Neither disease nor accident has claimed such a large percentage.

Unfortunately the couple usually experiences their grief alone. Well meaning friends, relatives, and even medical professionals may find it difficult to empathize and consequently they compound the problem by insensitive remarks. Alone, the woman felt the presence of a new life within; alone she now suffers the pain of unfulfilled expectations.

Frequently miscarriages and stillbirth are accompanied by feelings of guilt. "What did I do wrong?" "Why me?" Anger arises and doubt concerning God's goodness prevails. Medical explanations are not sufficient. At a time such as this, the couple needs both comfort and answers.

I have not seen any other book which has provided the personal insight and practical help that is offered here. Empty Arms is well researched and fills a great need. I'm confident that many struggling couples will find hope, comfort and encouragement in its pages.

Arnold L. Petersen II, M.D., P.C.

From My Heart to Yours

leven years have passed since the loss of our first child and the first edition of this book. Our lives have changed dramatically. John and I have been richly blessed with three beautiful children . . . and we've continued to learn more about trusting God in the dark. It's not been easy, but it has been good.

Since Empty Arms was first published, I have been flooded with letters from women across the country who courageously told me their stories and gave me the privilege of praying for them. I laughed and cried through the letters, feeling as if we had shared some of the deepest parts of who we were with one another. These memories I treasure.

Most of the letters came from women who had suffered a miscarriage or stillbirth, but there were also those that arrived from women who had survived a tubal pregnancy. They, too, had experienced great heartache, and some had even had a close brush with death. Many asked if I knew of any helpful resources about tubal pregnancy. Their need sparked the idea for a revised edition of Empty Arms which addressed the specific concerns of these women's heartache, and so this book has a chapter on tubal or ectopic pregnancy. I've updated information, written a new epilogue, and added a chapter on about letting go of our disappointments and pain.

It is my prayer that God will use the chapters ahead to meet some of your needs and to comfort you. If it were humanly possible, I would personally deliver Empty Arms to you so that I could be with you in your pain, gently squeeze your hand and offer you a fresh dose of hope and encouragement.

I'll likely meet only a small handful of those who read this book, but please, if we ever bump into each other, either here or in eternity, let's exchange a hug or two and talk about God's faithfulness to us as we braved our way along this path called life. Until then, it's one foot in front of the other, one day at a time, with our faces turned towards the Son.

Warmly,

Pam Vredevelt 1994

The Shocking News

I'm not picking up a heartbeat, Pam. There doesn't appear to be any fetal movement. I think the baby is dead."

In disbelief my emotions began to run wild and unchecked. Engulfed in a jumble of scrambled thoughts I wanted desperately to hear the doctor say, "Wait a minute— I'm wrong. I've made a mistake. Now I see the heartbeat." Those words never came.

During the next half hour in that little examining room, my life was a blur. Everything was out of focus. I hated my humanness. "Why can't I change this and make things different?" I thought. Somehow I wanted to say a few words and magically raise our baby from the dead.

Nothing made sense. Angry questions darted back and forth in my mind. "Why is this happening to me? To John? It's not fair! Thousands have abortions, but we want this child . . . why are we the ones to get ripped off? I hate this!"

The tears poured out. I sobbed long and hard, trying my best to listen to the doctor. He painted a picture of what might have happened: "Based on the measurements on the ultrasound screen, I can see that the baby is fully formed according to schedule, and most likely died just a few days ago. It's possible that the umbilical cord wrapped itself around the baby's neck. Or perhaps part of the placenta detached itself from the uterine wall. More information will be gleaned from pathology tests."

The doctor's words were overshadowed by my own thoughts: "I can't believe this is happening!"

Our day had begun in such a normal fashion. The alarm awakened us at 6:00 A.M. The leaders who help us pastor junior and senior high youth arrived forty-five minutes later for doughnuts and prayer. Our time together was one of closeness and warmth. As special prayer was offered for our baby just beginning its fifth month, I felt my love deepen for the child I carried.

By 8:00 A.M. the youth workers were gone and John left for the church office. Rather than going to work at the counseling center, I headed for my monthly visit with the doctor. I was excited about hearing the baby's heartbeat again. The fascination of hearing our child on the Doppler (a small amplification device used to listen to sounds in the womb) just four weeks earlier was still vivid in my mind.

The wait in the doctor's office was entertaining. A room full of pregnant women has always amused me. My imagination raced. "Will I really get that big in four more months? I wonder where she found such a beautiful maternity dress?"

Finally it was my turn for an exam. The usual blood pressure check and weigh-in were done first. "Hey, all right! Only one pound up from last month!" That was good news along with the nurse's words, "You're right on schedule."

The doctor was soon with me. Next came the moment I'd been waiting for. He said, "Let's listen to the heartbeat." It was like the first time all over again. I was so excited I embarrassed myself. After all, this was a common occurrence for the doctor. But for me, it was a thrill of a lifetime.

He placed the Doppler on my rounded tummy and gently searched for the baby. About a minute went by and my anticipation was at a peak. "Come on, Doc, let's get that thing in the right place.... I want to hear what this kid is doing in there!" I thought. The doctor explained that often the baby positions itself toward the back and this makes it difficult for the amplifier to pick up any significant sound.

A few minutes passed. Nothing was picked up by the Doppler. I watched intently for some cue as to what was going on. The doctor's face was blank. The nurse was stoic. I began to feel scared. What was happening? Confusion began to replace my excitement. The doctor very professionally explained that it would be best to take an ultrasound test for everybody's peace of mind before leaving the office. This would be a more reliable way of finding the heartbeat and checking on the baby's progress. I agreed and was moved to the next room where the test could be run. Apprehension lurked in the back of my mind as I entered a room filled with foreign instruments and equipment. My arms and legs felt like 200 pounds as I climbed up on the examining table. There I sat...shaken and chilled.

The nurse began to probe with the sound device to secure a clear picture of the uterus, placenta, and fetus. For what seemed to be hours it was unbearably quiet in that little dark room. I painstakingly blurted out, "Do you see a heartbeat? What are you finding? Can I see the screen?" only to be quieted with the remark, "I don't have a clear picture yet, Pam." More long drawn out minutes passed. Once again I bombarded the silence with, "Can't you tell me anything? Are you seeing a heartbeat?"

And then the ripping truth came. There was no heartbeat. The baby wasn't moving. Our baby was dead. What had gone wrong? The doctor didn't give a pat answer, but encouraged me that more information would be gleaned from pathology tests after delivery.

After delivery. Those words jolted me into reality. It would be necessary for me to go through the normal delivery process—but I would deliver a dead baby and go home empty-handed. It was all too incredible to grasp.

I had entered the doctor's office cheerful, bright, and anticipating the sound of life within me. I was leaving shattered, broken, and fearful of tomorrow. What would I have to walk through in the hours and days ahead?

Our Next Step: Delivery

I walked out of Dr. Petersen's office as full-figured as before, but with nothing to look forward to. The maternity clothes on the sewing table didn't need to be made. The nursery wallpaper wouldn't be hung. The crib we had on layaway would remain at the store. It was over. Our baby was gone.

I cried all the way home, embarrassed when other drivers looked at me. I felt like lashing out at them: "What are you staring at? Mind your own business!" My anger surprised me.

Anxious questions churned inside me. "What do I do next? Should I go to the church office and dump all of this on John? I don't want to ruin his day. He has important meetings tonight—maybe I should wait." Those thoughts were shortlived as I knew I needed John immediately, and he needed to know about his child. I was fearful about bumping into other people before reaching John. I prayed, "Oh God, please don't let John be busy with other people.

Please stop the phone calls. Please stop people from cross-
ing my path before I can get to him." In our line of work, the
answer to this prayer alone was a miracle.

Praying, I made my way to his office. I tried to be calm
but burst into tears, saying, "I have some sad news—our
baby died." He stood immediately and wrapped his arms
around me. With deep compassion he said, "That's okay,
honey—we'll have another one. It's okay, honey—we'll just
try again."

I'll always be grateful for those tender, loving words—
so simple, but so filled with hope. In the weeks to come
those were the words that gave encouragement in my darkest hours.

The rest of the day was one of tears and dependency on
each other. I never realized that I had the capacity to feel so
many intense emotions all at once. I was stripped of all
pride and accomplishment. Where other women had suc-
ceeded, I had failed in carrying a baby to full term. I was
fearful about what this was doing to my body. Did this
mean I wouldn't be able to have children later on? Would
my fertility be affected? I had only known one other woman
who had miscarried, and after three years she still wasn't
pregnant. Would this be true for me? I felt short-changed,
like a second-class citizen.

"If I can talk to Mom I'll feel better," I thought. I called
home from John's office, talking quietly so no one would
hear me crying. Mom's voice was a support in itself. I struggled to explain what had happened. She cried with me, and
asked if I wanted her to come to Portland. I couldn't even
give her an answer. I wanted her to come, but was so confused. I thought, "I'd be lousy company and might not feel
like talking." That didn't matter to her; she left on the first
flight the next morning in order to join us at the hospital
before the labor-inducing process began.

John and I spent the rest of the afternoon at home. We
tried to take a nap, but were too overwhelmed with emotion.

So we just lay there, held each other, and cried.

A long distance phone call from our pastor, Jerry Cook, interrupted our tears. At the time he was speaking in a conference in Calgary, Canada. His voice was compassionate, his words comforting and releasing: "Don't even try to be strong. Your tears are a natural response to your grief…that's the way you were built. Go ahead and cry." We were reminded that God had not left us. We felt grateful for the strong, life giving words Jerry had added to our hearts at a time when death was vividly fresh.

Soon after, another call came from some dear friends. Evie and Cal wanted us to come to dinner. They thought a good meal would help us keep up our strength. I didn't want to cook and we weren't hungry. Actually, neither of us knew what we wanted. So we went. It was a good choice. The family let us cry, gave us lots of hugs and support, and lent some big ears to our rational and not-so-rational talk.

Evie shared their experience of losing their first baby five hours after birth. I glanced across the dinner table at Keith and Dee Dee, their son and daughter, thinking, "God certainly made things up to them."

At 9:30 the next morning we arrived at the hospital. With a friendly smile the woman on the other side of the counter asked why I was being admitted. I said sheepishly, "For labor and delivery." In a loud, surprised voice she said, "But you're so little—you hardly look big enough to.…" Her eyes caught mine and with embarrassment I hung my head and replied, "I know—we lost the baby. But that's okay. You didn't know."

An orderly came to take me upstairs to the labor room. I hated this feeling of weakness. I was wheeled past the babies in the nursery. "This time," I thought, "I won't have the joy of seeing our baby through the nursery window. Maybe next year."

Within a couple of minutes, Beth came into the room to greet us. She was one of the nurses I grew to appreciate during this experience. She explained how labor would be induced during the next few hours and gave me a hospital gown.

I hated to put on that drab wrap. It reminded me of sickness and death. I felt vulnerable and powerless. I laid my head back on the pillow with tears streaming down my face and tried to assure John, "I'll be okay—it's just that everything is so new and scary." I resented the feeling of being out of control and helpless to change matters.

A sharp scream from a lady in hard labor next door interrupted my words of consolation to John. "Oh brother— do we have to listen to that noise for the rest of the day?" We turned on the radio—loud. Anything was an improvement over the grunts and groans coming from the lady next door! However, we did have a few good laughs over some of her expressions. At one point we laughed so hard that Beth stuck her head in the door and asked, "What's going on in here? Are you people having a party?"

It wasn't long before Beth came through the door again. This time my mom was at her side. It was so good to see Mom! Her bright smile and concerned eyes perked me up momentarily. We then broke down and cried together. Her presence was a tremendous source of strength to me. Over and over I thanked my Lord for a mother as wise as she. She didn't pop off with a single cliché. Pat answers such as "Oh, you're young—just look ahead," or "God knows best" were not part of her vocabulary. Instead, she laughed with us and cried with us. Every irrational idea we blurted out she patiently accepted. She let us feel to the fullest. She let us be, without expectations. Cords of love grew between us and bound our hearts together in a fresh way.

The inducing process began at 11:00 A.M. Another ultrasound picture again revealed no heartbeat and no fetal movement. This time the baby looked as if it were hunched over in a praying position. I caught a glimpse of an eternal perspective and thought, "Our baby is with the Lord, no longer tied to this world, but actually communing with God in His very presence. From the womb to heaven...not a bad life!" Those thoughts were short-lived. Loneliness with a longing for my baby soon clouded this picture of heaven. "Oh God...why couldn't you have shared this baby with us?" I thought.

Vacillating emotions marked the hours that followed. The nurses carried out their duties with tremendous sensitivity and compassion. Several times they stopped doing their duties, clasped our hands, and prayed for God to comfort and strengthen us. I was grateful for their loving care.

Over the next thirty hours, prostaglandin suppositories were used to induce labor. Contractions would come every two minutes but then stop. This went on for hours. I was weary. We walked the corridors to see if the exercise would stimulate more action. Touring the halls with Mom on one side and John on the other guiding the IV trolley—we were quite a sight. We reached an exit sign at one end of the hospital floor and John suggested we all run the stairs together! We laughed so hard that it seemed strong labor was bound to set in right there at the exit sign! No such luck.

Finally at noon of the second day, Dr. Petersen decided the cervix was "ripe" enough to do a D and C (dilatation and curettage) and felt the baby should be taken in this way. By this time exhaustion had wilted my body and my emotions were frazzled. Part of me liked the idea of being put to sleep and waking up with it all over. Part of me was angry. I wanted to see our baby!

Once again I felt cheated—what more was there to drain of my hopes and desires? I felt helpless; all confidence was completely knocked out of me. Nothing had been predictable during the past thirty hours. It seemed as though everything was out of my control...my body, my emotions, my thoughts. Instinctively, I listened to the professional counselor side of me. I diagnosed myself as a prime candidate for the psychiatric ward downstairs. I told Beth, "You may have to wheel me to the ward before they can discharge me as a patient in good health." She laughed with me, saying, "The confusion is normal. You're handling all of this much better than a lot of the women we get in here." It was good to hear that I was "normal."

John and Mom both thought I should finish the process by letting the doctor do a D and C. I trusted their judgment as I knew my immediate ability to reason intelligently was limited—to say the least! We signed the proper forms before the surgery and agreed to go through with it on one condition. We wanted to examine the fetus before it was sent to the pathology lab for testing. I wanted to see our baby no matter what it looked like.

Within the hour an orderly in his white coat wheeled me down to surgery. I talked briefly with the anesthesiologist and said a groggy thanks to Dr. Petersen for his medical care. Then everything went black. An hour later a recovery room nurse woke me from my sound, peaceful sleep. I didn't want to wake up. I wanted more anesthetic. I wanted to crawl back into that deep, dark sleep to avoid facing the world.

Dr. Petersen was by my side in a matter of minutes with a container full of the remains of my child. There really wasn't much for me to see—a lot of blood and pieces of tissue. He explained that the labor process and D and C caused the fragmentation of the fetus. Perhaps not seeing a fully formed baby made it easier to accept. I'm not sure. At that point I just felt numb.

I laid my head back down on the pillow feeling a tremendous loss. The grave reality of the experience penetrated the deepest parts of me. While it was comforting to know our child was with the Lord, the grief was intense.

My next thoughts came out in a whisper. "It's all over. I'm in the recovery room. The baby is gone. I'll be with John and Mom in a few minutes. It's all over."

Those words eased my mind to some degree and

helped me bear the pain of the hour. In one sense, it was all over yet in another sense, our challenges had just begun.

Chapter Three

Grief...the Road of Healing

One of the most difficult aspects of losing our baby was dealing with the emotional aftermath. The physical pain was acute at certain times, but temporary. Dealing with the many surfacing emotions was our greater challenge. Churning like a small tornado at unpredictable intervals, our feelings left us spinning in the dust.

For years we had ministered to others suffering grief. Now it was our turn to experience it. Although we would not have chosen the death of our baby, we did discover some tools during the healing process that helped us toward personal growth.

I realized quickly how unprepared I had been for the event! We had never suspected that this would happen to us. When the doctor said, "I'm not picking up a heartbeat or any fetal movement," all of my emotions gathered forces to shout, "NO!" I wanted to deny it. It was hard to comprehend that our baby was dead. There was no transition period. A few moments earlier I had thought I carried a healthy baby. I wasn't ready for the hard blow.

TEARS ARE HEALING

While counseling others, it was common for us to say, "It's okay to cry...tears are healing. The Lord made you with tear ducts for a very good reason...go ahead and let it out."

And that's just what we did. We cried until there were no more tears left. It might be encouraging for you to know that those tears continued off and on for weeks after delivery.

I remember one Sunday morning about four weeks later when John was sharing with the congregation the words to a song dealing with the power of God to "soothe our doubts, calm our fears, and dry all of our tears." He began to weep. Right there in front of God and 1,000 church people, he cried. God used John's vulnerability that morning in a very special way. Others who were hurting inside received strength and encouragement, and the tears were therapeutic for John as well.

Are you hurting? Then go ahead and cry! Cry hard, until the tears just won't come. This is not a time to try to be strong. Your grief will pass much sooner if you will allow yourself to feel and to express those pent-up emotions.

EMOTIONS MUST BE RELEASED

One thing John and I both knew from our studies on grief was that our emotions had to be released. If we stuffed them inside and squelched their expression, they would eventually come out in some other way on a physical or emotional level. The last thing we wanted to do was to set ourselves up for ulcers or fits of rage by pretending nothing had happened.

One of the worst responses you can have at this time is

to ignore or try to bury your hurt. A traumatic event is not nearly as damaging to you as how you react to it. This is the time when you'll be tempted to withdraw. The natural desire is to shrink into a shell and deny what happened.

Remember my experience in the recovery room when the nurse woke me up? I didn't want to wake up! I wanted the doctor to give me another dose of anesthetic to knock me out again. I didn't want to face reality. I wanted to crawl into my own little black hole and leave the world behind. This denial is a normal part of the grief process. However, it can be destructive if it is allowed to continue indefinitely. As a person denies, she also stops healthy emotional expression. If emotions are not expressed in healthy ways, they will be expressed in unhealthy ways. Turned inward, emotions can cause physical distress and sickness. Emotions unleashed inappropriately cause harm in our relationships with others.

This is where friends, family, and those supporting you can help. John and I played "Counselor/Counselee" with each other. He would vent his feelings; I would listen. I would share my thoughts; he would hear me out. We let each other cry.

There were times when I took risks to share my feelings. Part of me didn't want to be a burden to others. I knew, however, that each step I took to vent those feelings would bring me closer to the end of the grief process. So I determined to express those emotions. On days when I wanted to hibernate like a hermit I made myself talk or write. Sometimes I'd talk to John or friends. Other times I'd talk out loud to God. I'm sure that part of the time I made sense and part of the time I appeared half-witted. But it really didn't matter. The main thing was that I was expressing my surfacing emotions.

If it's hard for you to talk to others, or if you don't feel as though there are many you can confide in, start a journal. This is one of the best therapeutic tools available on the self-help market. A small investment in a spiral notebook will give you a place to unload all those feelings, irrational thoughts, deep hurts, and pleading prayers. One plus is that lined paper you're disclosing on won't talk back. The joy of a journal is that you can capture growth and progress on paper. If you start writing today, in two or three weeks you can reread your expressions and see how you've changed and progressed.

WORKING THROUGH GRIEF

During the days surrounding delivery, we were over-taken by extreme disappointment. Our dreams for our baby were shattered. The depth of this disappointment was hard for others to understand. It crept in like a cloud and just stayed there blocking out hope and happiness.

In the midst of our disappointment, however, we did experience points of relief. Here are some of the things that helped ease our burden and may help you, too.

First, in the midst of disappointment recognize that things will get better. The miserable feelings and hopeless-ness will be left behind tomorrow. You may not see this today, but in time you will. The extreme darkness will not hover over you forever. One day you'll be looking back on all of this. Focus on the parts of your life which have hope.

Second, recognize that grief is unavoidable and normal. It is a necessary process; the only healthy way to deal with loss. Dr. Elisabeth Kübler-Ross proposes that grief typically consists of five distinct stages: denial and isolation, anger, bargaining, depression, and acceptance of the loss. These may vary considerably depending on your preparation for the loss, extent of isolation or family support, belief in God, and so on.

It is possible that just when you feel acceptance settling in, you'll battle with another outburst of despair. Understand that unpleasant, painful emotions will come and go...sometimes in a flood, sometimes in a trickle. Realize that the change of moods you're experiencing now is natural and appropriate.

As C. S. Lewis commented after the death of his wife, "Grief is like a long and winding valley where any bend may reveal a totally new landscape.... Sometimes the surprise is the opposite one; you are presented with exactly the same sort of country you thought you left behind miles ago. That is when you wonder whether the valley isn't a circular trench. But it isn't. There are partial recurrences but the sequence doesn't repeat."[1]

At times John and I had to remind ourselves that the fluctuating emotions were to be expected. We were well acquainted with counseling tools and exercised therapeutic techniques legalistically: thought stopping, mood monitoring, praise, memorizing and quoting scripture, praying.... When irrational thoughts crossed our minds we challenged them. Sometimes we said, "That thought makes absolutely no sense whatsoever!" or, "That is a dumb idea and there is no evidence that it is true!"

When gloom descended sometimes we sang and other times we cried. We forced our minds to focus on the words of praise choruses and on worshiping God. John often played his favorite albums and filled the house with uplifting music. Sometimes this brought comfort. Other times more tears. But at least our emotions were being expressed.

I kept a record of my daily mood swings to see if my feelings showed any pattern. This monitoring showed lows in the morning and evening. To buffer those depressed times I made some alterations in my regular routine. In the morning I set the clock-radio alarm one-half hour earlier. I was awakened by Dr. Dobson's, "Focus on the Family" talk show. His comforting voice and the therapeutic content of his program seemed to focus my thoughts in a positive direction and help me cope. With a cup of coffee in hand, I wore off the morning grogginess about halfway through the program. This change in routine gave me some time to myself before facing the responsibilities of the hours ahead. I felt less rushed and more calm starting the day.

Since evenings were especially hard for me during my grief, I started scheduling in a regular Bible reading time at night. I had to specifically set aside time to do this. It wasn't always easy with the things left on my "To Do" list, but I knew I needed it. There were days when I just didn't feel like it, or care. Sometimes I read only ten to fifteen minutes. Other times I was able to enjoy a more leisurely reading period. Either way I received spiritual pick-ups that helped me cope with those low points of grief. Occasionally I squeezed in a bubble bath after reading to help me relax before going to bed. I struggled with some insomnia while my body was readjusting to a non-pregnant state. This new routine of slowing down my pace in the late evening helped me as much physically as it did emotionally.

Each of these activities was helpful. But in all honesty, there were still times when emotions raced in and out without any logical progression. We couldn't keep up with them. At those times we talked to ourselves out loud. We reminded our intellects that these grief feelings were normal. We weren't unspiritual to feel them. We weren't going off the deep end. We were merely walking through the normal grief process.

Third, realize that action is sometimes necessary for escape. I know—it sounds simplistic. But it works. You've heard the old saying, "It's easier to act yourself into a new way of thinking than to think yourself into a new way of acting."

Now granted, there were times when we didn't feel like doing anything! All we felt like doing was digging a hole and burying our heads in it. We forced ourselves to engage in meaningful activity as soon as possible. It worked best for both of us to go back to work four days after the baby was delivered. You may need more time; you may need less.

Whatever the case, do your best to protect yourself from withdrawal and structure profitable activities into your schedule.

The day I went back to my job as counselor at the counseling center, I didn't feel like going, but I knew clients were depending on me. That afternoon was marvelous therapy for me. In fact, I had some secret thoughts about writing checks out to my clients for services rendered! Forcing myself to go in to work that afternoon was beneficial in two ways. It took my mind off me and focused my thoughts and energies on my clients. It also gave my self-esteem an added boost. I discovered that not only was I still competent to counsel, but that I also had a new depth of compassion and empathy for my hurting clients that I had never experienced before. The discovery was uplifting and encouraging.

What do you like to do outside your home? What are some projects you've been wanting to tackle around the house? This is a time to indulge yourself! Do what you want to do. Plan some special things to look forward to. Schedule some time to tackle those "need-to-do's" around the house. Capitalize on your emotional energy and make it work for you, rather than allowing it to work against you.

One evening a week following delivery, we came home after a full day of work. I fumbled around in the kitchen trying to muster up dinner. The end result? Cheese sandwiches! Whoopee! Oh well, it seemed better than hot dogs! After dinner we spent our usual time together reading the Bible. The time was refreshing. But then unpredicted gloom returned. We sat in our family room moping and feeling terrible.

The idea of popcorn flashed across my mind. "That sounds good." I went to the pantry to get the popcorn popper, and two boxes and a pile of rags fell on my head. "What a mess! How did this closet get to be such a disaster?" I felt like laughing and crying at the same time (a rather frequent feeling during my grief). In this case, laughter won over the tears and John suggested cleaning the closet. This turned into one of those times when our emotional energies were channeled in a profitable direction.

Fourth, disappointment can be a catalyst for a renewed dependence on God. In your feeling of hopelessness, you can turn to the Source of encouragement and hope. He will show Himself strong on your behalf! When disappointment exploded inside, we longed for things to be as they were before our loss. No human being could diminish this hurt. Only God could offer comfort during these waves of disappointment and longing for our baby.

Our pain brought about significant growth in our lives. It deepened our dependence on and communion with God. We learned what it felt like to see no physical cure for wounds. Family and friends were helpful to a degree, but only God really knew when we suffered in silence.

If you are experiencing disappointments, remember this is a normal reaction to your loss. Allow God to intercept you at your deepest point of despair. To try to walk the road ahead by yourself will deprive you of a great experience with God. As you turn to Him in your weakness He *will* channel hope into your desert of despair. He will begin a new work in you!

It may not happen all at once. This new work will probably come in bits and pieces. It will come through circumstances and individuals God puts in your life. It will come through communion and sharing with Him. Remember, as a child of God you are *in process*. God continues to be your Father today, even when you don't feel His presence. You are His continual "workmanship" (Ephesians 2:10), and His piece of art. He will continue healing. He has not left you. He is at work in you, even now.

Chapter Four

Managing Anger

J ohn came bounding in the door for lunch one after-noon about three weeks following delivery. With a rather chagrined look on his face he said, "I had a weird experience driving home today. Something inside of me wanted to steer the truck into another car or tree—or anything!" We laughed together. I told him he was lucky there wasn't a hole in the front door. As I was coming in that morning with two arms full of groceries, the wind slammed the door shut in my face. This had happened before without affecting me in the least. This time I was ticked off! That stupid door—why couldn't it stay open for two minutes? I actually gave that door the kick of its lifetime! Fortunately I hadn't been lifting weights that week or we'd have had one more thing added to the fix-it list. We both chuckled and then discussed the anger we were feeling.

I had so many *why* questions. Why us? Why our baby when so many prayers had been offered on its behalf? If we had been cold toward God perhaps we could have under-stood. If we had been running from God maybe things would have made more sense. If we had despised God and His people, maybe we would have felt that we deserved this pain. But our relationship with God was good! We were loving and serving Him with everything we had. Why us? It seemed unjust.

I was angry with the injustice, and I was angry with myself. Several of my friends were enjoying pleasant pregnancies. They were succeeding effortlessly. "Why can't this body of mine do what it's supposed to do? I did everything Dr. Petersen ordered; why didn't things turn out for me?" I thought.

Our financial obligations also provoked anger. We left the hospital empty-handed, and now had a stack of bills! As with many families, our insurance didn't cover everything. Money we had set aside for household furnishings had to be forfeited for hospital costs. Anger accompanied our bill payments—what a rip-off!

ADMIT YOUR ANGER

One of the worst things you can do for yourself or for those around you is to keep that anger bottled up inside you. Anger must be released. Dealing with your anger openly and honestly will help reduce the intensity of the emotion. Pretending that it is not there only prolongs your agony.

Many of us fail to distinguish between *having* a feeling, *expressing* a feeling, and *acting* on a feeling. Identify the emotion and say, "I am feeling angry." This is crucial. It is not a sin to admit feelings of anger. It is a step in the right direction.

EXPRESS YOUR ANGER

After you have identified and admitted your anger the next step is to express it. But a note of caution: Anger is powerful; it can be extremely destructive or constructive. The result depends upon the manner of expression.

One way of expressing anger is to kick, swear, scream, and throw yourself into fits of rage. This will bring results, but you may find them less than rewarding! There are better options. Some people find it helpful to jog or do some type of aerobic exercise. My favorite anger outlet is the pool at our athletic club. I swim hard and fast, leaving emotional energy in my wake. Other women I know aggressively attack their kitchen floors with scrub brushes and their cupboards with sponges. You might try digging in the garden, running around the block, writing in your journal, or hitting your fist into a pillow.

I found it helpful to talk with John or an understanding friend. And it's always good to make your feelings a matter of prayer; tell God exactly why you're angry. Tell Him how you feel. He is not intimidated by your anger. He can handle it.

Ephesians 4:26 tells us, "'In your anger do not sin': Do not let the sun go down while you are still angry." There was a time in my life when I thought all anger was wrong and ungodly. A closer look at scripture cleared up this misconception. There are several Greek words that have been translated *anger* in the English New Testament. One of these is the Greek word *orgé*, meaning intense anger that comes as a reaction against sin or injustice. This is the type of righteous indignation that is referred to in Ephesians 4:26.

God endorses anger against injustice and sin. However, He also commands that in our anger we must be in control and "not sin." H. Norman Wright explains the ingredients of righteous anger.

The word angry in Ephesians 4:26 means an anger which is an abiding and settled habit of the mind, and which is aroused under certain conditions. The person is aware and in control of it. There is a just occasion for the anger here. Reason is involved and when reason is present anger such as this is right....

There are several characteristics of righteous anger. First of all it must be controlled, not a heated, nor unrestrained passion.... Second, there must be no hatred, malice, or resentment. Anger that harbors a counterattack only complicates the problem.... The third characteristic of righteous anger is that its motivation is unselfish. When the motivation is selfish usually pride and resentment are involved.... Another characteristic of righteous anger is that it is directed against wrong deeds or situations, not against people.... The final is that our anger ought to lead to positive and constructive action to right and wrong.[1]

The anger John and I felt was this type of anger. We despised the injustice of our baby's death. There was nothing fair from our human perspective about losing the life we loved from conception.

USE YOUR ANGER

If you have recently lost a baby, you're entitled to feelings of anger. Use your anger for your benefit. Let it work for you.

One positive function of anger is that it can be an energizer. It gives vigor and provides stamina when a task gets difficult. It enables you to deal with conflict by supplying the fuel for the fight. Use your anger to energize you into getting active and involved with people again. Use that emotional energy to fight against self-pity and withdrawal. When channeled your anger can be beneficial.

One of the motivators behind writing this book was anger. During the weeks following our baby's death I searched and searched for a book on pregnancy loss. The search was long and frustrating. Finally I found a secular publication dealing with miscarriage and it helped answer some of my questions. But I still had more concerns that the book did not discuss. So I set out to research and read through journal articles and quarterlies. This particular frustration and anger served as a positive function of energizing me to research for this book.

Another positive function of anger is that it can give you information. It can serve as a cue to tell you that it is time for you to begin to cope and deal with your inner feelings. As anger begins to build inside you, focus your attention on that surging energy. Ask yourself, "Why am I feeling this way?" Tune into those signals of anger. They can be helpful in working through your grief.

INSIGHTS ABOUT ANGER

In dealing with our anger it also helps to remember that we live in a fallen world. Bumps and bruises are all a part of this lost system. The notion that a Christian should never feel anger is irrational. We cannot live with one another without getting angry from time to time. I can't even live with myself without feeling anger once in awhile.

God's Word gave us further insight into how to deal with our anger. Consider the following verses.

Proverbs 16:32 "Better a patient man than a warrior, a man who controls his temper than one who takes a city." This shows us that it is better to control our anger rather than to let our anger control us. As practical experience illustrates, when anger gets out of control, matters get worse. A person tends to act before he thinks and behavior then aggravates the situation even further. Thus it's best to work at being "slow to anger." Proverbs 14:29 confirms this, saying, "He who is slow to anger has great understanding"(NASB).

James 1:19, 20 adds further insight with these words, "My dear brothers, take note of this: Everyone should be quick to listen, slow to speak, and slow to become angry, for man's anger does not bring about the righteous life that

God desires." As we studied these scriptures we realized we had a choice: We could deal with our anger in constructive ways and express it appropriately, or we could try to live in a make-believe fantasy world by denying the reality of our anger.

That afternoon when John came home for lunch we had a free-for-all expression of anger. No yelling or fitful rages occurred; we simply talked about our feelings. It lasted no more than ten minutes, but those ten minutes were tremendously therapeutic. The fires within us went from raging flames to smoking embers and we were able to face the rest of the day with peace of mind. Had we not dealt with the anger openly, John probably would have rammed a tree on the way home for dinner, and I probably would have kicked a hole in the door. Who knows? Fortunately, we never had to find out.

It is encouraging to remember that God knows us at every level of our lives. He understands our anger as a natural reflex and promises to help us move out of its crippling grip. He has committed Himself to give us the strength and endurance we need to cope with the angry pain of loss.

Untying Guilt's Knot

I f there is one thing I hate, it's feeling like a loser. And when I lost my baby that's just how I felt. I had failed. I despised my human weakness and inability to change things. All of this added up to one feeling: guilt.

Guilt feelings are common among parents suffering pregnancy loss. If you are among the majority of people who have lost a baby, you probably have been given few answers as to what might have gone wrong. Without answers, it's easy to become experts at concocting them. The result? More guilt!

After arriving home from the hospital, I searched endlessly for explanations. Did I push myself too hard? Was I under too much stress at the counseling center? Had I been too aggressive in exercising? Was I too sexually active? Had I eaten right? Did I skip vitamins? I groped for something to which I could attach the blame. This searching was unfruitful and only increased the guilt feelings. My agony was only compounded when, upon hearing about my miscarriage, one woman said, "I've been wondering if you've been eating right—have you?"

John carried a bag of guilt, too. Perhaps he had sinned and had disappointed God. Maybe God didn't feel he was ready to be a father. Could it be that he was being punished for past shortcomings? Maybe he hadn't prayed enough or was too ambivalent about the pregnancy. Though he knew the thoughts were irrational, they still prompted guilt which needed to be handled.

We also felt guilty about letting people down. Our parents were extremely excited about their first grandchild-to-be. My clients and our youth group had eagerly been awaiting the delivery date. We didn't want to tell them there would be no baby.

INSIGHTS ON GUILT

As a counselor, I have come in contact with other women experiencing guilt after losing a baby. Sharon describes her guilt in this way: "I felt so guilty after I had my miscarriage. Two years earlier I had had an abortion knowing I was going against God's will. When I found out I was pregnant, and really wanted the pregnancy, it was the greatest joy of my heart. But then I miscarried. I had felt certain that God had forgiven me for the abortion, but now I'm not sure. Maybe I needed to pay for my sin."

Sharon was feeling guilt common to many women who lose babies. However, since she is a child of God she has been forgiven. God did forgive her for the abortion when she repented of that sin. And because He forgave her, the miscarriage was not a "payment," for her past sin. God's forgiveness is unconditional. Once He forgives, He doesn't go back on His promise. To do so would be contrary to His nature. Psalm 103:12 tells us that in our repentance, "As far as the east is from the west, so far has he removed our transgressions from us." God is so good and loving that He paid the price for our sins even before we considered repentance. This forgiveness includes Sharon's past abortion.

A similar precipitating factor to guilt feelings after losing a baby is described by Cathy: "When I found out that I was pregnant, I was disgusted. It was a shock and I wasn't ready to deal with dirty diapers all over again. We all were happy with the way our family was and didn't like the idea of another addition. After a few months, though, we began to get excited about our 'gift from God.' Just when we had accepted the adjustment, our baby died in the womb. I felt certain that God had done this to punish me for my rotten attitude about the pregnancy."

Cathy's guilt experience is not uncommon, but her guilt was built on a false assumption about God. She felt that their loss was an act of punishment on God's part because of her "bad" attitude and ambivalence about the pregnancy. But God does not relate to us in this manner. We are not under the system of law and justice where we receive penalties and punishment for every wrong done. Christ's death on the cross has paid the price for our penalties. "He forgave us all our sins, having canceled the written code, with its regulations, that was against us and that stood opposed to us; he took it away, nailing it to the cross" (Colossians 2:13b-14). By recognizing punishment as an unnecessary premise for guilt, Cathy was helped to better handle the emotion during her grief.

DEALING WITH DOUBT-INDUCED GUILT

As we dealt with our guilt feelings, John and I had to recognize that there are things in life beyond our control. We are living in a fallen universe. Sin has and is corrupting our physical world. One outflow of this is death; another is unhealthy babies. In God's mercy a pregnancy loss can prevent the implications of the corruption of this fallen planet from being made manifest in certain babies. To feel guilty over losing our baby was false guilt. We were helpless to change the situation, so why should we feel guilty?

We also realized that doubt is not something to feel guilty over. We all have doubts. Our doubts about God's healing power caused tremendous growth in our lives. We were forced to ask tough questions. These questions drove us back into the Word of God for study and clarification about His character and will in our lives. Our faith increased as we began to face the hard issues of our beliefs.

You may be having doubts about God and your faith. Face those doubts head on. Don't pretend they aren't there. Search for some answers, then watch your faith grow. Some of the scriptural principles that strengthened our faith in God and His plan for our lives are these:

• Even though it's hard to see now, I trust that God will work something good out of this situation. "And we know that in all things God works for the good of those who love him, who have been called according to his purpose" (Romans 8:28).

• No matter what "hell" I have to walk through, God will be there with me. He never separates Himself from me. "For I am convinced that neither death nor life, neither angels nor demons, neither the present nor the future, nor any powers, neither height nor depth, nor anything else in all creation, will be able to separate us from the love of God that is in Christ Jesus our Lord" (Romans 8:38, 39).

• God will get me through this. "So do not fear, for I am with you; do not be dismayed, for I am your God. I will strengthen you and help you; I will uphold you with my righteous right hand" (Isaiah 41:10). God is with me even on the blackest days. "Even though I walk through the valley of the shadow of death, I will fear no evil, for you are with me" (Psalm 23:4).

• My God is also my baby's God. My baby just had the

privilege of seeing Him first. "Yet you brought me out of the womb; you made me trust in you even at my mother's breast. From birth I was cast upon you; from my mother's womb you have been my God" (Psalm 22:9, 10).

• God loves me and even though I don't understand it all, His ways for me are the very best. "All the ways of the **Lord** are loving and faithful..." (Psalm 25:10a).

• As I am patient, I will see more of God's helping hand in this loss. "I am still confident of this: I will see the goodness of the **Lord** in the land of the living. Wait for the **Lord**; be strong and take heart and wait for the **Lord**" (Psalm 27:13, 14).

• As I look to God for help, He will give me stability, joy, and security. "I have set the **Lord** always before me. Because he is at my right hand, I will not be shaken. Therefore my heart is glad and my tongue rejoices; my body also will rest secure" (Psalm 16:8, 9).

• God will lead us when we make decisions about another pregnancy. "I will instruct you and teach you in the way you should go; I will counsel you and watch over you"(Psalm 32:8).

• One way or another God will make children a part of our family and home. "He raises the poor from the dust and lifts the needy from the ash heap; he seats them with princes, with the princes of their people. He settles the barren woman in her home as a happy mother of children. Praise the **Lord**" (Psalm 113:7-9).

• God is on my side. "The **Lord** is with me, I will not be afraid...the **Lord** is with me; he is my helper" (Psalm 118:6, 7).

• God will see that what I need will be accomplished. "The **Lord** will fulfill his purpose for me" (Psalm 138:8).

• God knows me inside and out and accepts me 100 percent in this miserable state. "**O Lord**, you have searched me and you know me" (Psalm 139:1).

There are many other verses and chapters in the Bible that can bring comfort and renewed vision for your relationship with God. Allow your guilt and doubts to catapult you into a search for greater insight. You'll be pleasantly surprised by the growth this adds to your life.

SLOW-RECOVERY GUILT

About six weeks after delivery I experienced a different kind of guilt from those mentioned earlier. This guilt was tied directly to my physical condition. The doctor had said I would feel normal in about six to eight weeks. What was wrong with me? I was feeling dragged out and weary. Emotionally I was handling things well, but physically I wasn't; I was exhausted. In an effort to set new goals and engage in meaningful activities, I wore myself out. I was needing more naps to rekindle my energy, but felt guilty for not being more productive.

Part of the fatigue stemmed from the biochemical changes taking place in my body. My system was readjusting to a nonpregnant state. I later found that much of the exhaustion stemmed from anemia. When relief didn't come after cutting my schedule back, I had some blood tests performed. Sure enough, I was depleted of iron. I learned that anemia is common among women after a miscarriage or delivery. A healthy diet consisting of many raw vegetables, fruits, whole grains, and lean meat gradually built my body back to full strength. Prescribed vitamin supplements and a slower routine worked together to aid in my recovery.

I learned something from this experience: Exhaustion is not something to be ashamed of or to feel guilty about. It is my body telling me what I need to know. God has made our bodies in such a way that they desire to keep everything in balance. My fatigue was an alarm sounding off that something was wrong and needed attention.

THE OPTION OF MEDICATION

Following the loss of a baby, women suffer deep grief feelings and a sense of hopelessness. Depression and sadness are normal parts of the grief process. But there are those occasions when a woman may get stuck in depression and not be able to effectively do the grief work necessary to let go of her pain. Some women may have thoughts of suicide. Sleeping patterns are effected. There may be difficulty falling asleep, wakeful periods throughout the night, or wakefulness around four or five o'clock in the morning. This is accompanied by low motivation and low energy throughout the day, obsessional thinking, possible irritability, agitation, and perpetual guilt.

When these symptoms are pronounced, it is possible that a woman is dealing with a biochemical, clinical depression in addition to her grief. An anti-depressant can be very helpful in cases like this. An anti-depressant is not a pain pill that masks or takes away the hurt. It is a medication that restores the brain's chemistry back to normal so that an individual can effectively process all their thoughts and feelings. People who are clinically depressed get locked into a negative track and obsess over all the "bad" parts of their life. The chemicals in the brain that are responsible for regulating moods and allowing a person to switch channels of thought are depleted and need to be restored. Just as a pair of prescription glasses can restore a person's vision to 20/20, an anti-depressant can restore the balance of the mood-regulating hormones of the brain. This enables the person to do effective grief work and process all the different sides of their loss and eventually move beyond the pain.[1]

If you recognize any of the signs of clinical depression that I've mentioned, may I gently encourage you to see your doctor and discuss the option of a short-term use of medication. Many of the new seratonin specific anti-depressants are not addictive or habit forming, and they have few side effects. Just as the diabetic benefits from insulin and pneumonia patient is helped by anti-biotics, the clinically depressed person can be aided by an anti-depressant.

SUPPORT SYSTEM REDUCE GUILT

Some of my guilt was greatly reduced through talking with other people familiar with pregnancy loss. Hearing similar stories from other women, reading articles, and talking with those in the medical profession eased my burden.

One friend said to me in passing, "If the fetus couldn't handle your normal routine, it was not meant to survive." My doctor said that babies lost during the first four months of pregnancy are usually anatomically or genetically abnormal. Pregnancy loss is nature's way of screening out severely deformed babies. A nurse told me that nature didn't want me to have less than a perfectly healthy baby. All of these perspectives and opinions encouraged us out of guilt and on to a more hopeful outlook.

One way you can begin a support system is to get involved with people with whom you feel comfortable. You might consider your friends from church, family members, neighbors, or work associates. As relationships with others are cultivated, you'll be provided with emotional sustenance, tangible encouragement, further resources, and an enhanced ability to cope. Your support system will act as a buffer for you and help you reduce guilt and maintain equilibrium over time.

After we lost our baby, I heard about another woman, Donna, who had gone through a similar experience. I had known her casually from past youth camps that we both attended as leaders. We hadn't talked in over two years, but I decided I'd call her. That one phone call was followed by another half dozen conversations from which I received encouragement and strength. Since she had endured two miscarriages, she could empathize with my hurt and at the same time share information and resources with me. She was an invaluable friend!

At a time when the natural tendency is to hibernate and escape, let me exhort you to build a support system around yourself. Relief will come as you allow trustworthy friends to get inside your hurt. Risk it. You're worth it!

Spiritual Battles and Emotions

A s a counselor I recognize psychiatry and psychology as valid healing disciplines. I've invested years of my life and thousands of dollars toward becoming efficient in helping those with spiritual, mental, and emotional disturbances. Unfortunately, the Christian community at large is not comfortable with mental and emotional illness. As a result, people struggling with these types of disorders have often been pigeonholed as demonized (harassed or held in bondage by demonic forces). Grieving couples may hear others say that their bouts with depression are attacks from Satan.

A balance in our understanding needs to be reached at this point. "When we attribute the whole scene of mental and emotional problems to Satan, we remove personal responsibility for our choices and our behaviors. Satan gets the credit and we get an excuse."[1] For example, to say that all people experiencing chronic depression are demonized would be less than a balanced perspective. It would be better to distinguish be between spiritual, psychological, and physical depression.

During your grief you may experience one, two, or all three of these types of depression at a given point in time. Factors that could precipitate a primarily spiritual type of depression include true guilt, anger turned inward, a wrong perspective, and an attack by Satan. Psychological depression could occur in someone who, early in life, learned patterns ill equipping him to adapt to difficulties, or who was rewarded inappropriately as a child. Psychological depression could also occur when there is a thought disorder, when there has been a loss, and when false guilt is present. For you to feel depression over your loss is absolutely normal. Among the factors that could cause physical depression are hypothyroidism, hypoglycemia, biogenic amine imbalance, electrolyte imbalance, endocrine imbalance, fatigue, and viral illnesses.[2] If you lost a large amount of blood when the fetus was expelled, there's a strong possibility that part of your depression is a direct result of fatigue and physical weariness.

As Emery Nester has said, "We must face the reality of our imperfect psyches. We should look at imperfection the way we look at physical imperfection. At every period in life, we can develop kidney defects or heart difficulties.... Our mental conditions are imperfect as well."[3]

Because we live in a fallen world, we will have problems and struggles. Often these are a result of environmental and interpersonal conditions. There are times when our struggles are with the physical aspects of this world. In other words, the emotional upheavals we feel may be a result of psychological or physical causes. However, sometimes the causes may be beyond our humanness. Ephesians 6:12 tells us, "For our struggle is not against flesh and blood, but against the rulers, against the authorities, against the powers of this dark world and against the spiritual forces of evil in the heavenly realms."

In the book of Job, Satan is shown as one who watches over human affairs and searches out human weakness to make accusations before God (Job 1:6-11). Jesus refers to Satan as the father of lies (John 8:44). Satan is known as the accuser (Revelation 12:10), and he will do anything to make the believer feel condemned and guilty. He thrives on making us feel like losers.

Satan, the Christian's enemy (Matthew 13:39), is clever in his battle plan. Ephesians 6:11 tells us we must "stand against the wiles of the devil" (KJV). The word wiles depicts a very sneaky and crafty enemy. He is subtle and clever in the way he works against us. One of his common moves is to attack when the believer is weak and vulnerable. Few people are more vulnerable than the couple who has just lost a baby. As the tempter (Matthew 4:3), he delights in injecting our minds with ungodly thoughts; as the accuser (Revelation 12:10), he taunts us about being a terrible failure and disgrace.

Satan wants you to feel so crushed over your loss that you'll let go of your faith. He wants you to doubt God's love and faithfulness. He wants you to think nobody cares and that your suffering will never go away. He would like nothing better than to make you ineffective in every area.

Remember that Satan loves to scheme and devise ways to thwart God's purposes in your life. 1 Corinthians 14:33 tells us that God is not the author of confusion. When the Holy Spirit convicts a heart, he does so in a very specific, nonconfusing way. Satan's tactic is to cloud and baffle.

The word of God gives instruction as to how to deal with these supernatural influences on a believer. James 4:7 says, "Submit yourselves, then, to God. Resist the devil, and he will flee from you." This is a simple but effective battle plan. When trying to go to sleep one evening, I felt depressed and confused. I began to talk to the Lord about my feelings and James 4:7 came to mind. I realized that this heaviness and confusion was one of Satan's schemes to harass me and keep me from a good night's sleep.

How did I know this was the enemy attacking and not just some form of psychological depression? As I was praying, the Holy Spirit brought this understanding to my mind. The heavy feelings were vague and confusing. In the midst of these emotions I felt totally helpless, and saw no way out and no hope. I felt worthless and downgraded. Each of these is contrary to what I know and believe is truth. I know that with God there is always hope and help. In Him, I am not helpless. As a child of God I am also extremely valuable, not worthless. As I struggled with these feelings and talked to the Lord about them, I believe the Holy Spirit brought James 4:7 to mind to show me what I was dealing with and how to handle it.

I didn't want to awaken John, so under my breath I began to pray. I said, "Satan and all of your demonic forces, you are liars. You have no place with me for greater is He that is in me than you that are in this world (1 John 4:4). God has told me there is no condemnation for those who are in Christ Jesus (Romans 8:1), and the joy of the Lord is my strength (Nehemiah 8:10). I am in Christ. In the name of the Lord Jesus Christ, I command you to leave my presence."

The depression and confusion lifted and I was asleep in ten minutes. God is true to His word. When you call on God and turn to Him for help and stand firm against the devil, the devil must go! He not only goes, he flees in terror like a frightened dog with its tail between its legs. The power in the name of the Lord Jesus Christ cannot be thwarted.

Hebrews 4:12 says, "The word of God is living and active. Sharper than any double-edged sword...." It was the word of God Jesus quoted to Satan when He was tempted in the wilderness (Matthew 4). When confusion surfaced I used scripture time and time again to wage war. Sometimes the heaviness would disappear; sometimes I needed to deal with my emotions in ways already mentioned.

Another incident occurred when I was pregnant with

our second child, Jessie. After *Empty Arms* was published I received many wonderful letters from women across the country. On the day I turned eight months, I went out to my mail box as usual, and retrieved a letter from a woman on the east coast. She recounted her story of going in to see her doctor on the day her second baby was eight months along, only to find no heartbeat and no fetal movement. This triggered within me a flood of memories from our first loss and instantly I was filled with fear. If it happened to her, it could also happen to me a second time.

The rest of that week I couldn't shake the fear. I prayed, I sang, I journaled, I talked with friends, and tried all the diversions which usually worked, but to no avail. Finally on Sunday I was so tired of being afraid, I revealed my struggle to our pastor's wife after our church service. With a firm but gently voice she said, "I believe the enemy is harassing you with a spirit of fear, and I'd like to pray with you to break the power of that spirit."

We sat together on the front row of the church and she prayed a simple prayer: "In the name of Jesus, I speak against this spirit of fear and I stop all powers of darkness from harassing Pam."

That's all I remember because the turning point came for me after this first sentence. My fear was gone. As Diane prayed, I felt as if someone had literally untied the knot in my stomach. My mind stopped racing and returned to calm. God used this dramatic contrast between my struggle and victory to underline for me my need for others and to remind me of the power of His Spirit which is released when believers join forces together and pray. It wasn't enough to talk about my fears or to divert my attention from them. Prayer with another believer was what was needed to win the war against this fear.

Ephesians 6 is the believer's handbook on spiritual warfare. Acquaint yourself with the truth in these verses. Quote the word. When your struggle is one of a spiritual nature, the word will bring victory against attack; it cannot be broken. If, however, the heaviness and depression you're feeling is more psychological in nature, it's helpful to use some of the tools mentioned earlier for dealing with emotions. Add to those tools reading and memorizing the word, and you'll be on the road to wisdom, growth, and healing.

Let me close this section with these thoughts. In the midst of your heartache, it's better to pursue wisdom than to look for pat answers. Your emotional healing and growth will be a process, not an instantaneous event.

Chapter Seven

Responding to the Reactions of Others

Most people are uncomfortable with the subject of death. Conversation is frequently awkward and avoided. Those responding to the griever often experience the feeling we have when put on the spot—we don't know what to say, our minds go blank, and in an effort to say something, a sort of mumbo jumbo bursts out of our mouths. When our ears actually hear what was said, we want to crawl under a chair and hide. In embarrassment we're thinking, "That wasn't what I meant to say!"

Not everyone is familiar with the grief process experienced after a loss. Some people interpret continued sadness and depression as weakness or lack of faith. Because of this misunderstanding, grieving parents are susceptible to abrasive and flippant remarks. At other times responders are simply indifferent or evasive. As a result of those insensitive reactions, sorrowing parents sometimes find it easier to deny their feelings or to suffer in private.

BLUNDERS MADE BY MEDICAL PERSONNEL

In talking with women who had experienced pregnancy loss, I heard about many reactions they received from others. Some were positive. Unfortunately, many were negative. Often the insensitive remarks began in the doctor's office at the signs of impending loss. Communication with medical personnel was sometimes strained and artificial.

Donna shares her experience in these words: "My miscarriage started around 4:00 P.M. and by 4:30 P.M. I was hemorrhaging profusely. In that hour I called five times to talk to the doctor, only to be told that my call would be returned. I never received that call! My husband came home from work and there I was crying frantically, half-dressed, with blood everywhere. I felt stripped of all self-worth and demoralized. I tried my best to gather the remains of our baby in a container and we left for the hospital. I temporarily regained composure but then fell apart when handing the remains of our baby to the doctor. Anguish tore me apart as a nurse ushered me back to a small room.

"I was still bleeding heavily as the nurse fit me into stirrups on the table. I lay there with tears streaming down my face. Then in a cold, know-it-all voice the nurse said, 'Honey...I've had three of these. You'll get through it. In fact, I was glad about my last miscarriage because we didn't want more children anyway.' That was it! No sympathetic comments such as, 'I'm sorry you lost your baby,' or 'This must be very disappointing for you.' Only cold and calculated remarks that said in essence, 'Don't sweat it—it's no big deal.'"

Other women have suffered from similar insensitivities. Doctors often respond with avoidance, or with a "band-aid" approach (for example, suggesting to the couple that they forget it happened and to get pregnant as soon as possible). Several women said, "When my doctor told me I had lost the baby he didn't even look me in the eye—he looked at the wall instead." Another friend said, "Once my doctor detected there wasn't a heartbeat from the baby, he left the room and never returned. I think he found some excuse to flee so he wouldn't have to face me. I felt like I had committed a crime."

I came across several stories where other doctors had retreated from the "scene of the crime." Perhaps this withdrawal is used as a coping mechanism for feelings of failure and remorse over a patient's unsuccessful pregnancy. They may not know how to approach the patient. It helps to remember that a doctor is a human being with strengths and weaknesses like everyone else. More often than not, the obstetrician has been trained strictly in physical disorders. Grief counseling classes and training concerning emotional problems are generally not included in the physician's education. Regardless of the credentials behind a doctor's name, dealing with death and trauma can be as awkward and uncomfortable for him as it is for any other person.

Because of this, it is of utmost importance that the mother who has suffered a loss find a doctor and medical staff who can relate to her needs. It is the woman's responsibility and privilege to screen and choose a doctor she feels can relate to her as a person, not just as another name on the list.

I was fortunate to have had the excellent care of Dr. Petersen and his staff during my trauma. Sharon, the nurse running the ultrasound device, was the first to tell me that she couldn't register a heartbeat. She was honest and didn't inspire false hope. As my tears fell in her presence, she showed a great deal of compassion, saying, "We live in a fallen world and sometimes things we can't explain come our way. I'm sorry for you." Then she went on to explain how the doctor had just come back from delivering a three months premature stillborn and was really shaken and disappointed. After hearing of his sadness over another woman's loss, I instinctively trusted him.

While Sharon was talking, Dr. Petersen came in and looked for signs of movement on the ultrasound screen. Then he explained that he couldn't see any evidence of life. Handing me another Kleenex, he said, "I want to admit you to the hospital as soon as possible. I want to get you through the labor and delivery process so your suffering isn't prolonged." His eyes let me know he cared.

While I was in the hospital one of the aides in Dr. Petersen's office, Cathy, visited a couple of times to see how I was doing. She shared her story about losing a baby six months into pregnancy. All her words communicated that she was really "with" me and that she understood my heartache. Her bubbly smile brought sunshine into that little delivery room.

I'm grateful for Dr. Petersen, Sharon, and Cathy, and all those who helped me through those black hours. I regret, however, that many of my friends and acquaintances have not been as well supported by medical personnel. Mothers who feel that their present doctor is impersonal and unable to relate to them might want to consider another doctor better suited to meet their needs. Perhaps as more women communicate openly with their doctors about the trauma of pregnancy loss, there will be less denial and withdrawal and more sensitivity from medical personnel.

BLUNDERS MADE BY FRIENDS AND ACQUAINTANCES

Not only are blunders common among medical personnel, but they are also frequently received from friends and acquaintances. It's easy to start thinking that the "foot-in-mouth" disease has hit most of the people around you after a loss.

Chris shared about one incident she encountered: "When we found out I was pregnant we immediately started telling all our family and friends. We were so excited! When I called my friend, Carolyn, to tell her the good news, she said, 'Chris, you'd better wait until you're further along before you tell a lot of people. You could miscarry, you know.' It was hard for me to believe that she had actually said that to me. But in my excitement I just put it out of my mind. Then a few days after we lost the baby she said, 'I told you it would have been better to wait before announcing your pregnancy.' Again, I couldn't believe what I was hearing!"

Nancy shared a different story about her sister's reaction: "After I miscarried our baby, I went to visit my sister for a week. She is very expressive about everything. The whole time I was there she kept pumping me for details about the miscarriage and probing for reasons it happened. She told me to tell her everything and to express my deepest emotions. It was as though she thought I didn't feel bad enough about our baby and she was going to make sure I did. I resented that kind of pressure. There were times I wanted to talk about it, but there were other times when I didn't. I felt like telling her to back off."

John and I also experienced some difficult encounters. The evening before I delivered the baby a woman exhorted John with these words: "Several months into my pregnancy my doctor told me that my baby had no heartbeat and that it was dead. I didn't believe him and walked out of the office. My husband and I said a prayer of faith together and believed God to do a miracle. The next time I went back to the doctor everything was absolutely fine."

This story is a beautiful testimony of God's healing work in this particular family and we realize that she shared her experience with the motivation to encourage. During our grief, however, all we could think of was, "Why didn't God do that for us? Did God love them more?" We felt belittled and less spiritual.

Another response encountered by grieving parents is one that devalues and minimizes the importance of their unborn baby. Friends and family have never seen or interacted with the baby. To them there was little evidence of the baby's existence. It is therefore harder for them to discern the significance of the baby's death. Susan put it in these words: "My friends reacted to my baby's death like the death of someone they had never known. The impact of the loss was cushioned for them, and didn't seem to hold much value."

Outsiders rarely feel the impact of pregnancy loss as do the grieving parents. Because of this, comments such as, "Oh well, you'll have another one," or "Be glad you already have children at home," or "It's all for the best!" often find their way into conversations. These reactions are especially hard on a mother who has been physically and mentally involved with the baby from the first news of pregnancy. Barbie shared her feelings this way: "I got so angry with people who devalued my child just because it wasn't a full-term baby. They didn't feel it was that traumatic because they had never actually seen it. Some remarks from friends made me feel like I shouldn't be grieving so much...that my baby really wasn't a person, so I should move on with life and forget about it."

In our experience blunders happened mainly because people were uncomfortable with the subject. Comments such as, "Just look ahead—you'll have another baby," inspired some hope, but also left us feeling as though the individual we had conceived, loved, and lost was suddenly not supposed to matter anymore. It was impossible for us to dismiss it that easily. With certain individuals we felt as though we had to fight for the right to grieve.

Unfortunately, there are people in the Christian community who feel it is their duty to be God's special messenger to bring an "inspired word" to grieving parents. Sometimes these messages are destructive, more from man than from God.

We deeply appreciated our pastor's public response to our loss. The first Sunday we were able to be in church after the delivery, Jerry Cook spoke to the congregation, saying: "Many of you know that John and Pam were expecting a baby. That baby is now with the Lord... Now listen to me and listen well... They don't need any 'words from God' or 'inspired exhortations' or advice. They just need you to love them and hug them and let them work through their grief. There will be a point where sympathy will no longer be needed or wanted, so please be sensitive to them and just allow them to be themselves."

When we heard those words, a heavy weight was lifted from our shoulders. We felt released from other people's expectations and free to be ourselves. Expressions of love from the congregation brought healing and strength into our lives. Hugs came in floods. People prayed for us. Beautiful cards and letters came in the mail. Flowers perked up our living room. We were extremely fortunate to have been surrounded with such great support and encouragement. We counted our blessings!

Some families have not been so fortunate. Sharon shares a destructive reaction she received: "After my second stillbirth I was totally devastated. My hopes had been extremely high since I carried the baby to full term. After the baby's death a lady came up to me in church and said, 'Before you get pregnant again it would be a good idea to search your heart and make sure you've gotten rid of all the sin in your life."

Marion received a letter with another blundering reaction:

Dear Marion,

The Bible teaches us that what a person sows he will also reap. I remember you telling me that you had had an abortion several years back. Maybe with this miscarriage you have reaped the disservice you sowed years back. No doubt your payment has been paid. The Bible says, "An eye for an eye and a tooth for a tooth." Most likely your next pregnancy will go just fine as you continue to serve the Lord with all your heart.

Sincerely,
Rachel

I came in contact with Marion shortly after she received this message. The letter had done nothing but compound her agony, leaving her feeling more devastated than before. Not only had Rachel completely misapplied a scriptural principle, but her insensitivity was also unchristian. Fortunately, Marion understood the scriptures well enough to know that the letter was misdirected. It's sad the way some pour salt in a fresh wound.

THINGS TO DO WHEN BOMBARDED BY BLUNDERS

Similar blunders were easy to find among the women I interviewed. In an effort to help myself and others buffer these insensitivities, I devised the following reminders and posted them on my refrigerator door. You may wish to do the same.

• Assume the best in those responding to you and realize that their intentions are usually not malicious. "Love bears up under anything and everything that comes, is ever ready to believe the best of every person..." (1 Corinthians 13:7 Amplified Bible).

• Realize that careless remarks usually come from ignorance and lack of understanding. If your friends have never experienced a pregnancy loss, it is very difficult for them to know how to relate and how to respond. Be patient with them. "Love is patient" (1 Corinthians 13:4).

• Many people respond to death in general by denial, so expect some people to react to your baby's death this way. Even though it isn't the healthiest response, sometimes it is the only response they know. Make allowances for them. "I urge you to live a life worthy of the calling.... Be completely humble and gentle; be patient, bearing with one another in love." (Ephesians 4:1, 2).

• Accept the fact that there will be people who will want to give you advice. Some will feel they have an inspired message from God about your baby. If the advice is encouraging and in line with scripture, be encouraged! If it is condemning, realize that it probably wasn't "heaven sent."

• For the insensitive reactions that do hurt your feelings it helps to remember Christ's example: "When they hurled their insults at him, he did not retaliate; when he suffered, he made no threats. Instead, he entrusted himself to him who judges justly" (1 Peter 2:23).

• Resist all tendencies to hold a grudge or bitterness in your heart. This will only magnify your anguish and pain and prolong the grief process. "See to it that no one misses the grace of God and that no bitter root grows up to cause trouble and defile many" (Hebrews 12:15). Even though forgiveness isn't always easy, it's always best.

You Can help Your Friends Respond Appropriately

There are some things that you can do to make it easier for your friends to respond to your needs. The old saying, "honesty is the best policy," is a good principle to live by.

Your friends can't read your mind concerning what you need or want; only you know how you really feel. *Force yourself to express exactly how you're feeling and what you would most appreciate from them.* For example, Renee called me a couple of weeks after delivery. She said, "I just want you to know that if there is ever a time when you want to talk, I'm just a phone call away." On that particular day I was feeling blah and didn't want to talk. I said, "I really appreciate your call, and there probably will be a day when I'll want a listening ear, but I just don't want to talk today." She was receptive and open hearted. A few days later we talked in her office; our time together was uplifting and encouraging to me. She told me she appreciated my honesty.

If it's possible, try to initiate some of the contacts with your friends after your loss. It is natural for them to have mixed emotions and awkward feelings about how to approach you. If you approach them it can break the ice. It will also help them feel as though you need and want their support.

When we first heard our baby was gone, I called Mom right away. The whole family called back a couple of hours later and my sister, Kelly, expressed her mixed emotions. "I wanted to call you earlier but I just didn't know what to say." She started crying and continued, "I feel so bad, but I don't know what to say, or whether I should have called or anything…" I assured her that just hearing her voice gave me a boost and that I was glad she called and wanted her to call again and again. The first step had been taken and she was a great support.

Sometimes it's a good idea to excuse yourself from a difficult situation. There may be times when you'll find yourself in the middle of a discussion about babies, babies, and more babies. If this is difficult for you during your grief, politely excuse yourself. Assume that your friends will understand, and allow yourself some breathing space. It's best to be yourself. If you feel you need to leave, go ahead and realize that it's all right to feel that way. It's a normal part of grief.

Several weeks after our baby died John and I vacationed at a ski resort in the Northwest with four other couples. Two of our close friends brought their newborn baby. We were fascinated with their infant and with watching them in their new roles as mom and dad! One evening the men went into the living room to watch a televised football game. The rest of us stayed in the kitchen girl-talking and eating popcorn.

At one point the conversation turned to babies and children; I was the only one without either. Loneliness for my baby started welling up inside. So I opted for the football game with John and the guys. Actually, I think I "covered" the move by saying I wanted to serve the guys some popcorn and 7-Up. The change of scenery helped and I had a chance to regain my equilibrium. These friends understood my needs for both companionship and privacy.

When you are feeling strong and positive, lead into conversations about your loss with a positive approach. Your optimistic overtones will set the stage for interactions with family and friends. Renee expressed it this way: "When we realized we were losing the baby we talked everything through and felt as though we had a pretty good outlook on the whole situation. I didn't want to call our parents because I knew it would hit them harder than us. However, when I did call, I explained what was happening and reassured them that we were doing well and had optimistic plans for the future. By approaching them at a time when we were relatively 'up' and positive, it helped them handle things easier than if we had approached them during one of our 'low' points. Our attitude set the stage for their response."

Another way to assist friends who want to help is to give them specific suggestions as to how they can help you. Cathy and I organized some suggestions to give her friends after her stillbirth experience. (These ideas were adapted from Wendy Bergren's practical pamphlet "Mom Is Very Sick— Here's How to Help.")

- Come and visit me at home. Please call first so I can "pull my act together" before you arrive.

- Ask if you can drive my children to their little league practice.

- Ask what favorite meal we would like to have and fix it. My energy level isn't high enough to be creative yet. I'll supply the ingredients!

- Offer to help me with some of the ironing. Standing for long periods of time is hard for me. It will be a joy to see my husband leave for work in a nicely pressed shirt.

- Tell me it's O.K. to be sad around you. This will release me to experience the grief process in honesty and protect me from denial and withdrawal.

- When we talk about my loss, refer to my loss as my baby, not as some unknown "it."

- Don't avoid me. I need you to communicate with me. If I want to talk about my baby, don't change the subject.

- Tell me you think I look beautiful even if my face is pale and there are circles under my eyes. I need that perspective because right now I feel less than attractive.

- Pray for me, and tell me specifically how you are praying. This will build me up spiritually.

- Invite me to go out. Don't assume I'm not able to do so. If I feel too weak physically or too down emotionally, I'll tell you. Chances are I'd love to join you.

- Tell me about yourself and what God is doing in your life. This will give me more faith.

- Ask me if I'd like you to come for an evening to "do nothing." It's nice having someone around when the rest of the family has other obligations away from home. If I need the privacy, I'll tell you. If not, we can enjoy each other and a bowl of popcorn.[1]

You may have other ideas concerning ways your family and friends can help you. Be honest and specific with the people who ask to help. When people want to serve you, receive their expressions of love—don't reject them. And if people aren't offering help, ask for it. It won't be easy. But as you honestly share your heart, you will be enriched, others will be blessed, and you'll progress through the grief process.

Chapter Eight

Husbands Hurt, Too

I n the course of suffering a pregnancy loss, the married couple often feels wadded-up, thrown down, and trampled on by life. The shock of a loss often jolts the husband as hard as it does the wife, leaving both partners on an emotional teetertotter. The most common feeling among husbands during a loss is one of helplessness. Even though they want desperately to be supportive, they feel powerless.

John put it this way: "After I found out about our baby's death, I kept wanting to do something to make things better, to change things. But there was nothing I could do to give our baby life again. I couldn't alter our baby's destiny and was frustrated by being so helpless. All I could do was be with Pam and support her in whatever way she needed me. So I canceled meetings and spent the next two days with her in the hospital. During the thirty-six hours of labor I felt even more helpless. I wanted to do something to speed up the process. I even found myself angry with the doctors for not making the delivery end faster—as if they had some magical control over the delivery time. I was frustrated being powerless to control the situation.

"During the weeks that followed I felt helpless in other ways. I remember one afternoon thinking that Pam was back to her normal optimistic, level-headed self. That same evening she burst into tears when she dropped an egg on the kitchen floor! I felt helpless in my inability to make everything all right. I later realized that it was unrealistic to expect immediate emotional healing. There were a lot of ups and downs for both of us, and it wasn't fair for me to impose my timetable for mourning onto her."

Other men not only feel helpless, but they also have tremendous difficulty watching their wives suffer. Queasy stomachs are common when a man cannot stand the sight of blood. Tom's experience depicts one reaction known to many husbands. "The alarm went off at 6:30 A.M. and we woke up in a pool of blood. I almost vomited. Neither of us knew that Cathy had been losing the baby through the night. We're both sound sleepers, and we were shocked to find our bed soaked in the morning. The last time I saw blood like that was in high school when I gashed my leg with a saw. The thought of it makes my stomach churn even now.

"I took Cathy immediately to the hospital and by that time she had started cramping. I'd never seen her in such extreme pain before. I hated it. I wanted to take the pain away from her. It would have been easier on me to bear the pain myself rather than to watch her suffer like that. By the end of the morning I was wasted."

Helplessness and queasy stomachs are not the only common responses among husbands. Oftentimes they feel baffled and befuddled at what is going on. Impossible to prepare for, a crisis often leaves the husband confused and dismayed. Michael summed this up well: "When Renee started spotting I really didn't give it much thought. I had not heard much about miscarriage so the idea that we were losing the baby didn't cross my mind. We talked about what was happening and were basically positive. Then Renee began hemorrhaging and losing large amounts of blood. I was uncertain as to what to do. I didn't know if she wanted to be alone or if she wanted me to stay with her. I was concerned about her and the tremendous blood loss. She kept telling me that she was okay, but somehow I found that hard to believe. I vacillated between wanting to be with her and wanting to let her have privacy. I was perplexed and didn't know what to expect. This was a whole new experience for both of us."

Shortly after I had returned to work at the counseling center, a woman called who had suffered two miscarriages, the most recent eight months before. She and her husband were experiencing marital problems stemming from their losses. "I don't know how much longer I can take his cutting remarks. He keeps blaming me for losing our baby and for not being more careful during the pregnancy. I did everything the doctor told me to do but we still lost the baby thirteen weeks into pregnancy. I can't convince him that it was not my fault, or his fault, or anyone's fault. It just happened."

During the grief process there is often a desire to find someone or something on which to pin the blame. This can be extremely damaging to the marriage relationship. It is not constructive in any sense. Blaming each other, or yourself, will only complicate matters and intensify your problems. Even medical science doesn't have definite answers as to why pregnancy losses occur. It is therefore destructive to assume a cause and to heap guilt and blame on the other partner.

In a society where "macho" men are idolized, sensitivity is often viewed as a sign of weakness. Husbands, many times, are caught between their desire to be supportive and understanding and their desire to be strong and secure. Is it okay to feel upset? Am I being less than masculine in hurting right along with my wife? Shouldn't I keep a stiff upper lip and grin and bear it? What are normal reactions at a time like this? It might be releasing for you to know that on the average, men and women often experience the same intensity of grief.

A husband needs to know that as a male he is not alone in experiencing intense emotion. Thousands of other husbands have had the same feelings in their losses. It is also good for the wife to know that often her husband experiences depths of grief similar to her own. I've heard many women say, "My husband just can't relate to my heartache—he doesn't feel it as deeply as I do." Chances are that he does feel deeply about the loss but doesn't express it in the same ways. An absence of verbal admission doesn't necessarily demonstrate an absence of grief. Sometimes grief is simply being swallowed.

A magazine of obstetrics and gynecology included the following chart which shows the similarities husbands and wives share in their grief reactions.

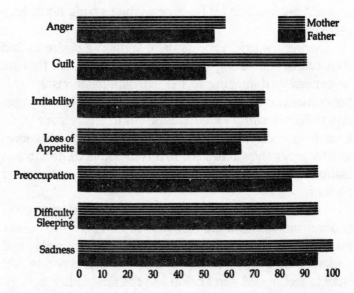

Each bar represents the percentage of subjects who indicated that the item was a problem after their baby died.[1]

THANKS...TO HELPFUL HUSBANDS FROM WIVES WHO HURT

Many men I talked with were frustrated by their ignorance about how they could help their wives. What could they do? In an effort to diminish the unknowns, I asked wives to share positive ways their husbands supported them during their times of grief.

• Even though you felt useless at the hospital, thank you for staying with me as the loss occurred. When you rearranged your schedule to walk through the trauma with me, your presence reminded me that I am loved.

• When you made adjustments at work to be home more often during the weeks following our loss, it showed me you cared. Thank you for not burying your sorrows in your work by overscheduling and keeping busy.

• Several weeks after our loss it helped me to know that you weren't pushing me to "get over it." Thank you for not expecting me to be instantly normal, or even back to my old self after months had gone by. God knows how hard I was trying to move on with life. If you had condemned me for not being on top of things, I would have been even more depressed. Thank you for releasing me from those expectations.

• Even though it was hard to talk about at times, it meant so much to me when you shared your feelings openly. I grew to love and understand you in ways I never had before. Thank you for being vulnerable with your emotions.

• Some people try to ignore their problems, thinking they'll go away. Thank you for forcing yourself not to forget it all. Because we faced what happened, we grew together rather than apart.

• There were so many days I was up and down on a roller coaster of emotions. It helped me when you didn't assume that what I said was what I meant! Sometimes I didn't know what I wanted. I'd tell you I wanted to be alone, but I really wanted you to hold me close. Thank you for being extra sensitive and double-checking with me about my needs.

• Right after our loss I wanted to hibernate. I didn't want to see anyone and was content to be a recluse. It helped when you took the initiative to get me out of the house. Going for a drive or out to dinner to a private and quiet restaurant brought relief to my sorrow. Being alone together away from home helped.

• When I went back to the doctor for my post-delivery visit, it was like reliving everything again. Thank you for being available to talk when I came home. Your phone call from the office asking, "How did it go and how are you?" made the blows easier to bear.

• Our calendar is always full of engagements. It helped me when you were protective and shielded me from sensitive situations. When you asked, "Honey, will it bother you to go to so and so's house? They have a newborn and two little children," it took pounds off my shoulders. There were some days it wouldn't have bothered me, but there were others when it would have been difficult to hold a rational conversation. Thank you for taking the lead in declining engagements that I wasn't strong enough to handle.

• There were times when I didn't have the physical or emotional energy to give quality attention to my other children. It helped me so much when you voluntarily stepped in and grabbed the kids to play with them. Watching you read to them or wrestle with them brought me great joy.

• I gained great strength when you stopped to pray with me a couple of minutes each day. I looked forward to those times because there were moments when I was so confused I didn't know what to pray aside from, "God, help!" Three months after the miscarriage you said, "I'm praying for you to have a great day today." I can't tell you how much those little prayers meant even after you thought I was "back to normal."

• When I was feeling guilty about the stillbirth, you did not blame me in any way. I don't know how I could have coped if you had communicated that it was my fault. Thank you for reassuring me over and over again that it was nobody's fault, that it was a part of human suffering known to this world.

• Above and beyond everything else, it helped me to know that you loved me at a time when I felt extremely unloveable. Thank you for all the ways you expressed your love. From the "I love you's" to the rosebuds in a vase, I received strength and encouragement to go on with life.

Husbands and wives need to support and encourage each other during times of pain and stress. When one partner tries to suppress or deny his grief, the pain is only intensified. Let me exhort you to be open and honest with each other. Don't hold up expectations. Let your partner know how to help you. Allow your grief to bond you closer together as a couple.

Chapter Nine

Helping Children Understand

The nurses let my five-year-old son, Teddie, come in and see me a few hours after I delivered." He had begged and begged and although young children are not usually allowed this privilege they finally snuck him in to me.

"He crawled up on the bed, threw his arms around me, and gave me the biggest kiss I'd ever had. Then these loving words came: 'Mommie, I know you're sad about my baby brother, but I've come to make you happy again. I even brought you your favorite cookies,' and he pulled out a package of Oreos. I'll never forget those precious moments.

"After the miscarriage was over, I was lying in the hospital bed feeling numb. I think I was still in shock. My sister-in-law, Nancy, and Alexis, my three-year-old niece, interrupted my fuzzy daze as they entered the room with a bright bouquet of spring flowers. Alexis came over to my side and clutched my hand. With a serious and puzzled

look on her face, she said, 'Aunt Donna, where's the baby?'
I began to explain to Alexis in words I thought she could
understand: 'Alexis, my baby is with Jesus. When the baby
was growing in my tummy, something went wrong and the
baby died. But the baby is with Jesus now and won't have to
have any more pain or hurt or ouchees.' Then with a concerned look, she asked, 'Is the baby happy now with Jesus?'
I assured her and said, 'Yes, Alexis, the baby is very happy
with Jesus.' That's all she needed to hear and her response
was, 'Well, that's all right then,' and she dropped the subject."

When a miscarriage or stillbirth occurs, it is not only the
baby and the parents who are affected. Children in the family also feel the sting of the loss and experience their own
type of grief. They really do understand that something
called *death* has happened. They may not understand every
aspect of the situation, but one thing they do know—Mom
and Dad are acting differently this week than last week.
They're more grumpy. Mom cries a lot and Dad doesn't talk
as much. When his parents are in the blackness of grief, a
child can feel confused and alone. Questions creep into his
little mind such as, "Did I do something wrong? Do
Mommy and Daddy still love me? Why did my baby sister
die? Will I die, too?"

TALKING ABOUT DEATH

Some parents I have talked with in counseling feel the
need to protect their children and to shelter them from the
subject of death. When the family dog dies they quickly go
out and buy another dog and say to their children, "Spot ran
away, but we have a new dog now that will be your pet."
This may soften the blow to the child grieving over his for-
mer pet, but it does nothing to help the child come to grips
with a natural part of life...death.

I remember distinctly a couple of incidents that happened to me when I was in the second grade. My normal

routine was to feed my goldfish before leaving for school. One morning when I went to the fish tank, all three of my fish were floating belly-up, dead. Running to Mom with tears streaming down my face, I cried, "My fish died! My fish died!" Mom explained that death was a normal part of life and that she was sad, too. She asked, "Would you like another goldfish?" My immediate thoughts were, "But what are we going to do with the dead fish?" As it turned out, we flushed them down the toilet since "they would be most comfortable in water anyway." Mom had a new fish waiting for me that afternoon.

The very next day my four-year-old brother was playing with his pet frog and I was making a miniature barbeque grill with sticks and stones. I stood up to get some more rocks and his frog jumped in front of me without my seeing it. My foot landed right on top of it. My brother started wailing at the top of his lungs, "You killed my frog!" We both were devastated and ran crying to Mom.

As she picked up the remains of the frog, she said that she would take care of it for us, but my brother stomped his feet and protested. Through his tears he said, "But we have to have a funeral first and bury him!" He obviously didn't want to pretend that nothing had happened.

Four pets dead in one week! Now that was a lot for a seven-year-old and a four-year-old to handle. But good lessons were gained as Mom talked openly with us about death. She didn't ignore our sorrow or make up some wild tales about fishy and froggie heaven; she simply discussed death in a loving and matter-of-fact way so that we could learn from those experiences.

I share these simplistic stories to emphasize the extreme value of openly discussing the subject of death with your children. They will adjust to your grief in a much more healthy manner if they understand why you are sad and are assured that they are not the cause of your sorrow or the cause of the baby's death.

SHARING YOUR LOSS WITH YOUR CHILDREN

One of the best things you can do for the other children in your family is to talk about your miscarriage or stillbirth. One of the worst things you can do in front of the kids is to ignore the subject and pretend it never happened. No matter how old or young the children in your family are, they do sense that something has happened. That much they know for sure! If explanation and open talk are not provided for them, they will use their imaginations to fantasize possible causes for Mom and Dad's different behavior. These imaginations and fantasies are usually more harmful to the child than would be an open discussion of what has actually occurred. Bobby, an eight-year-old, said it in these words: "Mom and Dad are so different. Dad doesn't play with me as much. Mom yells more. They don't talk much either. I can't figure out what I'm doing wrong. No matter how good I am, I can't make them happy. Maybe they just don't care about me any more. That's why I stole the candy. I wanted to see if they would do something. Before, Dad would have had a long talk with me if I had done that. I wanted to talk. But he just spanked me and sent me to my room. I don't think they love me as much as they used to."

Kelly, a nine-year-old, reacted to her parents' grief in a different way. She tried to cope by withdrawing. "I like to stay in my bedroom alone. It's nice in there. I have my friends [stuffed animals] with me and they're always happy. They don't yell at me or ignore me. They play with me whenever I want. My bed is there and my soft blanket. It's all nice. Besides, all Mom and Dad want is a new baby."

Before children can cope with death, it is necessary for them to understand it and to have their questions and fears addressed. if death has not been a topic of discussion in your family, here are some guidelines you might find helpful.

It's okay for your children to see you cry. It teaches them that life is full of both joy and sorrow. When you cry, tell them that you are sad about the baby and that crying helps get rid of sadness.

Don't say to your children, "Don't cry ... it will be okay." This will teach them that crying is wrong. Allow them to cry right along with you. They need that emotional release, too.

Set a time to explain what has happened. Choose a time when you feel emotionally strong. You will have ups and downs, so pick one of the more optimistic times to have a talk with the kids. Both parents should be involved in this.

Use simple terms to describe the situation. For example, if a miscarriage occurred, you might want to say something like this: "Mom and Dad went to the hospital two days ago because the baby was having problems. The baby's problems got worse and when we got to the hospital we found out it had died. The doctors think that the baby wasn't growing right so that's why it didn't live. We feel sad about the baby's dying, but we are so glad to have you with us and we love you very much. So if Mom and Dad are sad or grumpy, it's because we're sad about the baby. We're not mad at you or unhappy with you. We're just disappointed that we couldn't bring the baby home like we brought you home from the hospital when you were born."

If you experienced a stillbirth, one way you can approach this discussion is by using the baby's picture taken in the nursery and some of the other keepsakes you may have collected. This will give your children something tangible to identify with and it makes it easier for them to understand. Sally shared a story about the way Beth, her six-year-old, handled their stillbirth: "When Beth saw the baby picture and footprints of Aaron she got all excited and exclaimed, "That's my baby brother! I want to show my friend's mommie... I know Aaron has gone to heaven, but he's still my baby brother! Can I take Aaron's baby book to school tomorrow and show Mrs. Anderson [her teacher]?'"

Use this experience to teach your child that death is a normal part of living in this world. You have a good opportunity to implant a lifelong lesson in his heart right now—use it. As you discuss things openly, you'll be drawn closer together as a family.

When you speak about the death of your baby, refer to it as "death." Don't refer to it in fantasy terms such as, "the baby has gone away" or "the baby went to sleep and will never wake up" or "the baby has become an angel." These explanations will only confuse the child in the long run. When you want to convey the idea that the baby died, say "the baby died."

Simply explain what happened to the baby after it died. If you are a Christian, this part of the conversation can teach your child spiritual truth that will bring great encouragement. You might want to say something like this: "Susie, when you were born into this world, you were born with a body and your person lives inside your body. Your body is just a shell or an outside covering for your person on the inside. You have a healthy shell or a healthy outside covering. When Shelly was born, she didn't have a healthy body. But she was still a person on the inside. Shelly's body died at birth, but her inside person is in heaven now. The Bible teaches us that when our outside body dies, our inside person goes to be with God in heaven. And that's where Shelly's inside person is now. Her body is in the grave at the cemetery, but the *real* Shelly is with God in heaven. We all will miss her, but someday we'll all get to see her in heaven."

It is wise to guard against saying things such as, "God took the baby to heaven." In a child's mind, that might cause unnecessary fears about the possibility of God taking

Mom and Dad to heaven now, too.

Disarm fears and guilt in the child's mind by stating that the death was nobody's fault. Often children have imaginary but very real fears and guilt when confronted with death. One of the best ways to prevent this is to deal with it head-on.

Eight-year-old Mike shared in a counseling session: "When Mom and Dad said I was going to have a baby brother or sister, I was mad. I didn't want anyone else in the family. I was going to have to share my room and didn't want to. Maybe the baby died because I was so mad and he knew I didn't want to share my room. Did I make the baby die?"

Unnecessary guilts and fears can be alleviated with an explanation such as, "The baby's death was nobody's fault. It died because it wasn't healthy enough to live and its body wasn't strong. Its death wasn't your fault or Mom's fault or Dad's fault or anybody's fault. There was nothing any of us could have done to make it live. The baby simply wasn't healthy enough to survive."

Expressing her fears about sickness and death, Tarah said: "I never want to get sick again. I never want Mom or Dad or David to get sick again. Mom and Dad said that the baby got real sick and died. If I get sick will I die, too?"

Tarah needed to be reassured that sickness does not automatically mean death. A fuller explanation that the baby wasn't only sick but that it also had many other problems will help. The more that is communicated, the less room there will be for unfounded fears.

Reassuring words are good to use consistently if you detect any fear or guilt responses in your children. One of the best ways to find out how they are feeling about the situation is to ask them. Simply say, "How are you feeling today about the baby?" If they are unable to answer a question that general you might ask, "Do you feel sad about the baby?" or "Are you upset about the baby?" Then let them describe what they're feeling. It might take awhile for them to get it out, but often a patient and listening ear will get an answer.

Be generous with affection. At a time when your children see you sad and up and down emotionally, they need constant reassurance that you love them. Give them verbal assurance daily. Let them hear you say, "I love you," time and time again. It will help buffer the storm.

It is also good to be generous with hugs. Sometimes younger children will not be able to understand the changes they are feeling in the family. But they'll always understand a big bear hug and a kiss! Be aggressive with affection.

If you feel that your child is not adjusting well to the loss, don't be reluctant to seek help from a professional counselor. A counselor can help you determine how your child is adjusting and give you support in helping him through the grief process. Many people seek help during grief and this can add stability to your lives. Your need is legitimate!

One encouraging thing to remember about children is that they are extremely resilient. They bounce back quickly after a hard knock from life—oftentimes better than adults. If communication, love, and affection are openly expressed in the family after a pregnancy loss, all family members will be strengthened and helped. A trauma can do one of two things: It can drive your family apart if you close communication and build walls, or it can pull your family closer together if you open communication lines and build bridges of love between one another. My prayer for you is that your trauma will serve to cement your relationships and build appreciation in your hearts for those special family members God has already given you.

Chapter Ten

Please...
Someone Give Me
Some Answers

O ne of the most difficult challenges for me to deal with after my miscarriage was the unknown. I kept wondering what was happening to my body. What did all of this mean for our future family plans? Was this loss affecting fertility? Why had I carried a healthy baby one day, only to find out that it was dead a day later? I was in the dark and had many fears.

One of the best ways to reduce fear is by gathering facts. Ask questions and pool answers regarding your concern. Proverbs 11:14 says, "Where there is no guidance, the people fall, but in abundance of counselors there is victory" (NASB). Bit by bit, peace did come as I received answers from skilled people in the medical field. Here are some of the questions I asked and the answers I received.

MISCARRIAGE

"What is a miscarriage?" was the first question I wanted answered. I had never been confronted with the experience before and had very little understanding of the term. A miscarriage, or spontaneous abortion as it is called by physicians, is, I found, the premature spontaneous delivery of a fetus before it is able to live apart from the mother's womb. This will usually happen before the twentieth week of pregnancy.

Medical doctors told me that there are several types of miscarriages as shown below.

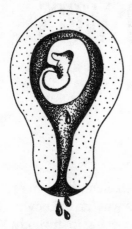

Threatened abortion. This term is used when a woman bleeds and cramps, but the cervix is still closed. The process could stop and the pregnancy continue. One-half of the women who bleed and cramp early in pregnancy do not miscarry.

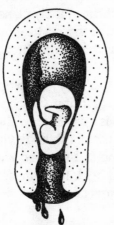

Inevitable abortion. When bleeding becomes heavy and continues for several days, and if the cervix opens and severe contractions occur, this term is used. The process has progressed so far that it is no longer a question of whether or not pregnancy will continue.

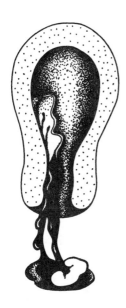

Incomplete abortion. A complete abortion occurs when the uterus has expelled all of the fetal and placental tissue. An incomplete abortion occurs when some of the tissue is still inside the uterus. In some cases even though the fetus has died it is not immediately expelled.

Missed abortion. This term is used when a fetus dies at least four weeks before being expelled. The fetus will often be expelled in bloody clumps of tissue or early in pregnancy as a small embryo.

Habitual abortion. This term is used when a woman has had three or more consecutive miscarriages.

The Commonness of Miscarriage

I also wanted to know how common miscarriages were. Before our loss, I had never talked with anyone about the experience of miscarriage. I felt alone and wondered if this was something that happened to many other women, or if I was one of few to go through this. I found out that miscarriages are said to occur in 20 percent of all pregnancies. Medical professionals estimate the number to be even higher when taking into account the unreported losses and those that occur within the first weeks of pregnancy and are undetected. Generally, one of four pregnancies ends in some sort of a loss, whether it is miscarriage, stillbirth, or newborn death.

One doctor explained the commonness of pregnancy loss to me this way: "In the animal world 50 percent of all offspring born are early abortions due to some kind of abnormality. If we were to add up all the unknown losses and the reported and unreported miscarriages in human experience, the statistics would probably be close to the 50 percent loss of the animal world."

Proneness to Miscarriage

After our loss I had some fear about the possibility of miscarring again. Was I more susceptible to losing a baby than others?

Scientific research has shown that a woman's chances of having a miscarriage depend on several factors. If you have had one miscarriage already, the likelihood of having another one is the same as any other woman, i.e., one out of four. The possibility increases to four in ten if a woman is over thirty-five, took six months or more to conceive, and/or has had previous miscarriages. Moreover, if you have had two previous miscarriages your chance of having another one increases slightly from one in four to one in three. There is still a strong chance that you will carry a full term baby if you get pregnant again three chances against one. And a woman who has suffered three or more miscarriages has a fifty-fifty chance of carrying a baby full term.[1]

TIMING OF MISCARRIAGE

It seemed strange to me that my baby could be growing and progressing right on schedule and then all of a sudden die. Did other women carry babies for four months and then lose them? When did other women experience their loss? I found that medical studies show that 75 percent of all miscarriages occur within the first twelve weeks of pregnancy. My loss was part of the 25 percent experienced later in pregnancy. It encouraged me to know that if I were to lose another pregnancy, it was more likely to occur early in pregnancy rather than later.

CAUSES OF MISCARRIAGE

Why did my baby die? What caused our loss? These were my most pressing questions. Dr. Petersen was very helpful in explaining some of the possible causes. He shared with me that miscarriages occurring early in pregnancy (during the first twelve weeks) are thought to be due to abnormality in the fertilized egg or in the process of its implantation in the uterus. The fetus may be deformed because of genetic problems inherited from the parents, but more often a chance mutation or problem has occurred during fertilization or early growth of the embryo. If the fertilized egg does not undergo normal cell division, the body works in such a way to rid itself of the abnormal tissue and early delivery occurs. Abnormal cell division is not the fault of either parent. It is merely one of the many mishaps that occur in the genetics of human experience.

Dr. Petersen also explained to me that miscarriages

occurring later in pregnancy (after the twelfth week) are thought to be the result of problems in the baby's attachment to the placenta or uterus. He pointed out that there may also be structural problems in the uterus itself. It is also possible that an "incompetent" cervix can prevent a full term pregnancy as it is too weak structurally to hold the fetus and dilates prematurely.

Dr. Paavo Airola, a nutrition expert and educator, discusses some other factors that have been linked with causing miscarriages: cigarette smoking, poor nutrition, exposure to environmental pollutants such as toxic chemicals and radiation, contraction of a serious disease or infection during pregnancy, and drug usage.[2]

Medical science doesn't have pat answers for the causes of all miscarriages, but Dr. Petersen explained that there are several factors that are not scientifically documented to be causes: exercise and physical training during pregnancy, sexual intercourse during pregnancy...no matter how active the couple's experiences are, a previous miscarriage, emotional problems or nervousness, birth control pills used prior to conception, IUD (intrauterine device) used prior to conception, and psychological shock.

Knowing this information helped dispel some of the misconceptions and fears I had concerning our loss. It was a relief to have some answers to the many questions swimming in my mind. As the "unknowns" decreased, I felt more peace.

STILLBIRTH

Although 75 percent of all pregnancy losses occur during the first twelve weeks, there are still many people who experience their baby's death late in pregnancy. The longer a baby is carried, the more devastating the loss can be for the parents. I felt Don and Jackie's intense despair as they shared their story with me: "My pregnancy had gone smoothly. I exercised daily and felt great having gained only the twenty-five pounds needed. By the ninth month I was getting uncomfortable, though, and I wondered if the baby was ever going to come. One week past my due date I started getting anxious and two weeks later real fear set in. This was our first baby and I couldn't understand why it wasn't coming on schedule.

"Finally, contractions started on a Thursday afternoon. Don rushed home from work to take me to the hospital. He was so excited! The week before we had completed the final touches on the nursery and everything was ready for the arrival of our baby.

"Labor was long and hard, but normal. The doctor came in for the final examination and said I was dilated to nine and just about ready to give birth. Our moment of glory had arrived! It was really going to happen—we were having a baby!

"The nurses wheeled me into the delivery room and the doctor slipped on his sterile gloves to help with the birth. From that point on everything moved rather slowly. Contractions were intense and my pushing was hard but the baby just didn't want to come. At last the doctor was able to help the baby's head out, but his ashen face told me something was wrong. The nurses scrambled around the room, calling for help from the nursery. Something wasn't right.

"There were no shouts of excitement from the doctor and nurses. No one said, 'It's a boy' or 'It's a girl.' The baby was loudly silent. The doctor quickly handed it to the nurses. Our baby was blue...and not breathing. Don and I just looked at each other numbly. Working furiously, the nurses labored over our baby, but their attempts at revival were futile. Our baby had died during birth. The umbilical cord had wrapped around his neck in the birth canal and cut off his oxygen supply. Our baby was gone. The doctor came over to us after doing all he could to help our baby and said, 'I'm sorry. The baby didn't make it...I'm just so sorry.'"

Don and Jackie's story illustrates some of the feelings and events that can occur during a stillbirth experience. It is one of the most difficult and trying experiences a couple can ever walk through. As with couples suffering a miscarriage, those experiencing stillbirth have many questions.

In a pursuit to offer Jackie and Don emotional support after their loss, I came across some information that helped them understand their experience. One question I needed answered for myself was, "What is a stillbirth?" I discovered the term *stillbirth* is used to refer to the delivery of babies that die in the womb after the twentieth week of pregnancy, or die during labor and delivery. The fetus usually is more than one pound in body weight. This is different from a "neonatal" or newborn death which is defined as the death of a liveborn infant at any time during the first twenty-eight days of life.

CAUSES OF STILLBIRTH

Jackie and Don were similar to John and me in that they desperately wanted some answers to *why* their loss occurred. If you have suffered a stillbirth, you probably have been given little information as to the "whys" of your baby's death—and you probably find little consolation in the answers that are provided. Because the research on stillbirth is limited, the answers are limited. The information is just not available.

Medical research shows that in up to one half of all stillborn deaths, the cause of death is never determined. There are some factors, though, that scientific researchers feel contribute to the causes of stillbirth: the compression of the umbilical cord during delivery; the wrapping of the umbilical cord around the baby's neck during labor and/or delivery; the premature detachment of the placenta from the uterus, the contraction of toxemia, high blood pressure, or diabetes during pregnancy; the presence of severe abnormalities in the baby; and an abnormally stressful or prolonged labor and delivery.

Although this information did not lessen the intensity of Don and Jackie's emotional pain, it did assist them in understanding their experience. This understanding helped them, as it did me, to deal with many of the misconceptions and fears attached to their loss. It disarmed fantasies and aided them in coping with their grief.

Undoubtedly this is a time when many painful questions are filling our thoughts. Even when answers are available, trauma is difficult to endure. In most cases perplexing questions outweigh available answers, intensifying grief's penetrating blow.

This chapter was intended to be only an overview of some of the medical information available on pregnancy loss. Other factors are more fully discussed in medical books such as those listed at the back of this book.

Let me encourage you to be assertive in searching for answers to your questions. The more you can reduce the unknowns by gathering information, the less room there will be for fear, worry, and misconceptions.

Chapter Eleven

After a Stillbirth

A s I talked with women who had suffered a stillbirth, I was shocked to hear some of the hospital experiences they encountered. I was grateful for my positive experience, but I grieved with them over their heart-rending nightmares.

One of the most agonizing parts of many women's deliveries was not knowing what happened to the baby after delivery. Sherry shared her story with me in these words: "I lay on the delivery table as the doctor sewed me up. The nurses had taken my baby to another room. I hadn't even seen her yet. The doctor wasn't talking. All I knew was that something was very wrong in all of this. When he was finished stitching me, he left the room. There I was all alone in that cold, sterile delivery room. My husband wasn't with me because of Air Force duties. No one was there. I remember hearing my crying echo off the four bare walls.

"The doctor came back in a while later and said, 'Your baby is dead. The nurses are tending to her and will carry out the necessary procedures. You don't need to concern yourself about those things now.'"

"I had no idea what he meant when he said the nurses were carrying out the necessary procedures. Everything inside me cried, 'I want to see my baby! Whether she's dead or alive, I want to see her!' When I asked the doctor if I could hold her he said, 'Everything is being taken care of for you. We'll take you back to your room now so that you can rest.'

"I felt guilty for asking to see my baby. It was as though I had said something out of the ordinary in asking to hold her. I never did see her. I never had a chance to say good-bye."

It was hard for me to imagine the pain Sherry endured that day! Fortunately, cases like Sherry's are happening less frequently. Hospitals and physicians are becoming more in tune with the psychological needs of parents who have experienced a stillbirth. If you have suffered a stillbirth, there are some specific things that will be helpful to consider while in the hospital.

SEEING YOUR BABY

Even though your baby is dead, he or she is still your baby. You have the right to see and hold him. Doctors and nurses will usually comply with such a request.

Some parents are afraid to see their stillborn babies, especially if they have not dealt much with death and dying in the past. If this is the first member of their family to have died, or if they have bad memories of funerals, it may be hard to think about viewing their own baby dead.

I have come across couples who have chosen to see and hold their stillborn baby and couples who have chosen against it. Brenda and Mark discussed their experience with me: "We knew our baby was dead, but we both wanted to see him. He was still a product of our love and we wanted to have some time with him before the funeral. The doctor said he was not deformed in any way and just looked like he was asleep. The nurses brought him to us and then left the room so that we could be alone. We held him and cried, and held him and cried. He had a miniature version of Mark's nose and my mouth. It was hard to say good-bye to Mark, Jr., that day, but it would have been more difficult for us if we hadn't had that time alone with him. It helped to know he was a perfect baby. It gave us a slight hope for another perfect son in the future."

Susan had different feelings after her delivery and she chose not to see her baby. She told me about her feelings, saying: "I couldn't bear to look at my dead baby. When the doctor asked me if I wanted her brought to my room, I said, 'NO!' The thought of it nauseated me. It was hard enough to think about her being dead. How could I see her? I wanted to remember her differently. I didn't want to remember a dead baby in a pink blanket. I just wanted to forget the whole thing."

Two months later, Susan regretted her decision not to see and hold her baby. She kept wondering what her daughter looked like and if she had any of Susan's features. Guilt gripped her for not wanting to hold her baby. "I didn't even say good-bye to my own daughter."

If parents take the opportunity to be with their baby before leaving the hospital or before the funeral, these struggles can be eliminated. This, however, is a decision that the parents have the right to make on their own.

You may wish to ask the doctor or nurses to describe your baby to you, as did Brenda and Mark. In reflection they said, "When the nurse described his appearance we wanted to see Mark, Jr., even more. She kind of paved the way for us and made us more comfortable about the idea of spending time with him."

BABY PICTURES

If the doctor or nurse has described your baby to you and you still are not sure if you want to hold him, you do have the option of asking them to show you a picture of your baby. Sometimes photos are taken by the hospital for records. If this is not standard procedure, you can ask them to supply you with a picture; most hospital staffs will honor this request.

Whatever is best for you is best for you. If it is too difficult at this time for you to look at a baby picture, then don't. In a few months, if you feel like you can look at your baby's picture, you can always ask your doctor to show you the photograph in his records. Most important, you do whatever you are most comfortable doing.

Building Precious Memories

During the thick of your grief you may be saying, "This is one experience I want to erase from my memory." It is normal to want to remove the pain and hurt and suffering you are feeling now. But you will never forget the special son or daughter that was born to you. He or she will always be a very real and important part of your memory.

One way that some couples have magnified the precious side of the memory of their baby was to make a baby book. They used it as a tool for explaining to other children in the family about "baby brother" or "baby sister." It gave the children and the parents some physical points of identification and helped them understand the experience more dearly. If this sounds like something you might want to do, here are some things to consider including in your baby's book.

- the picture taken in the hospital nursery

- an explanation of the labor and delivery

- a lock of hair

• a set of footprints

• a birth certificate

• the baby's arm bracelet given for identification in the nursery

• a small scrap of paper from the final monitoring showing a tracing of the child's heart rate

• a record of the weight, length, head, and chest measurements of your baby

• a piece of the baby blanket your baby was wrapped in

• the baby's death certificate

• cards and letters written to your family concerning the baby

• dried flowers from bouquets given to you

• a copy of an announcement sent out to family and friends of the baby's birth and death

• the doctor's explanation of why the baby died

• scripture verses that helped you during your suffering

• poems you wrote or that others gave you about your baby

• comments made by others that offered encouragement and hope.[1]

You can talk with your nurse about some of these items.

In most cases the hospital staff can help you record this information before leaving the hospital.

The Autopsy

A few hours after Don and Jackie delivered their still-born, their doctor came back to talk with them about doing an autopsy on the baby. In talking with medical profession-als, I found that doctors usually want an autopsy performed to see if they can find out the cause for the baby's death. Some parents refuse because they have unpleasant feelings about their baby being subjected to that. It seems clinical and insensitive. For others refusal stems from religious beliefs. But some families find hope and encouragement for future babies from autopsy reports. If the condition of the baby is found to be normal, then there's absolutely no rea-son why another normal baby couldn't be birthed without delivery complications in the future. An autopsy report can alleviate many feelings of uncertainty and guilt.

When I talked with Don and Jackie about this, my first question concerned what was actually done in an autopsy. They explained to me the information their doctor had given them: "An autopsy is simply a careful examination of the baby's internal tissues and organs. If a stillborn baby shows no physical deformities externally, an autopsy can help determine whether or not there were any internal mal-functions or problems."

Don and Jackie went on to explain that many hospitals have a pathology laboratory where autopsies are per-formed. "Our baby was taken to a lab located in the same facility in which I delivered. However, some hospitals per-form autopsies at another location if they don't have a pathology laboratory." I realized after hearing this that some women might have the big frustration of not knowing where their baby was taken. If I were in this situation, I would definitely want to know what was happening with my baby! It might help for you to know that it is your right to know where your baby is and that the following questions are appropriate for you to ask medical staff:

- Why do you want to do an autopsy? Should one be done?

- When do you want to do it?

- Where will it be done?

- When will I find out the results of the tests?

- How much will the autopsy cost?

- After the autopsy, can we pick the baby up and take him to the funeral home or should we have the mortuary attendants take our baby from the lab?

FUNERAL ARRANGEMENTS

As a counselor and a pastor's wife, I am frequently called to help comfort people when they lose loved ones. I know that at a time like this most people need as much emotional support as possible. One way to receive this support is by working with a funeral home in planning for the baby's burial and memorial service. Funeral home personnel are usually very sensitive to grieving families and will do their best to help you with all the details. Before you finalize the funeral arrangements, it may help to consider the following concerns:

- Do you want to be involved in making the arrangements or do you want another family member or friend to do it for you? Would you want them to make decisions without checking with you first? (Sometimes problems can develop later on if you are excluded from planning the funeral.)

• Which funeral home is the most convenient for you to visit as you make plans for the funeral?

• Is there a funeral home with which you are familiar and feel comfortable?

• If you are uncertain which funeral homes are available in your area, check the Yellow Pages or ask friends for a recommendation. Doctors and nurses may be able to give you some suggestions of good services available, too.

• Ask the cost for the baby's funeral.

• Find out if transportation of the baby is provided from the hospital to the mortuary. Ask, "How much will this service cost?"

• You will need to decide whether to have an open or closed casket ceremony.

• If you have a church that you attend, you might want to consider a memorial service with your pastor or minister officiating. Funeral home staff will work with you at the church if you desire.

• If you choose to have a service at your church, inquire about the costs involved. Generally there will be a slight charge for the minister, for any musicians you would include, and possibly for the use of the building. Your pastor or minister will be able to give you these figures.

Saying the Last Good-byes

One of the most beautiful stories I've heard of a family saying good-bye to their newborn was that of Joyce and Pat. Their perspective is inspiring and their family was drawn closer together as a result of this time shared together. Joyce tells the story: "We had the memorial service at our church. It meant so much to us to have the people in our congregation with us when we said our last good-byes to Jennifer. They were so supportive.

"Before the service began, Pat and I held Jennifer one last time. She looked like a perfect angel, sound asleep and content. The staff at the funeral home had allowed me to dress her in a pretty white, ruffly dress that Mom and Dad had given us the week before she was born. She looked precious. Pat took a picture of her to help us remember how beautiful she was.

"Our two other children held her a couple of minutes before the service, too. They wanted one last chance to say good-bye. Kevin, our six-year-old, brought his little stuffed dog and said he wanted Jennifer to have it with her in 'her bed' (the casket). It was a sad time, but a time that drew our family closer together. We grieved together because we all missed her. But we rejoiced together because we all knew she was with God. Some day all five of us will be reunited once again."

If you have suffered a stillbirth, let me encourage you that the important thing to remember about saying your last good-byes is that it is your time to do whatever you want to do. You might want to consider some of the things Pat and Joyce did in their last good-bye. You may not feel comfortable with the ideas mentioned. That's okay. Do what is best for you and your family. The ideas set forth in this chapter are simply to help you become aware of more options for dealing with your personal situation.

Chapter Twelve

The Challenge of a Postpartum Body

A bout six weeks after our loss, I remember sitting in the jacuzzi at our athletic club after a competitive game of racquetball. The friend I was talking with asked me how I was doing. Drained and red-faced, I said, "Well . . . some days it's a harder grind physically than emotionally and this is definitely one of those days!"

It takes time for emotions to heal and for feelings to work through the grief process; it also takes time to physically regain strength. Sometimes I felt this was unfair. Just when my emotions seemed to be stabilized I was faced with the physical reminders that what I'd once expected was absent.

After delivery, your body undergoes some definite, but normal, changes. These are the same changes your body would make if the baby were taken home from the hospital. As a result, there are several challenges that accompany your post-delivery days. I know that I was encouraged when I discovered that what I was experiencing was normal and common to many women.

POSTPARTUM BODY CHANGES

After my miscarriage I wanted to know what I should expect to experience physically in the weeks ahead. More crucially, I needed to know that what I was dealing with was normal. Sharon, my nurse, helped me to understand that my body didn't realize that my baby had died. All my body knew was that I used to be pregnant and now I wasn't. It would be adjusting back to a nonpregnant state.

I learned that a discharge called *lochia* usually continues for approximately two weeks after delivery. I was instructed to change a pad every few hours. My nurse said, "Gradually the discharge will diminish and turn brown. If you attempt too much strenuous activity before you have healed inside, there is a possibility of hemorrhaging. So take it slow for a couple of weeks. Allow yourself to relax." I was also told to call the doctor right away if any heavy discharge began after it had been progressively diminishing.

My friend, Cathy, had to deal with not only the discharge, but also with her breasts filling with milk. She had lost her baby in the sixth month. All her body knew was that it was supposed to be preparing for nursing the baby who was no longer in her womb. Her hospital nurses gave her some information as to how to stop the milk from continuing to come in. They said, "Try to do everything possible to keep your nipples from being stimulated. Close fitting bras that do not rub are helpful. When you bathe, wash around the nipple rather than completely over it. Every little precaution against stimulation is helpful. It may be uncomfortable at times because of the extreme fullness in your breasts. An over-the-counter pain reliever or ice pack can be helpful in tolerating the discomfort. The aches and pains are very normal and to be expected."

Another friend of mine handled the coming of her milk in another way. She had a toddler at home who had not been completely weaned and he was able to nurse. Gradually her milk diminished. This alleviated full breasts and helped lower her level of discomfort.

After their stillbirths, Susan and Karen experienced odd sensations every now and then of the baby kicking in the womb. This happened to Susan as long as three months after delivery. Encouragement came when their doctors told them that these sensations were common after a stillbirth. There is no reason to become alarmed when the sensations occur. For some women this is a natural part of the body's adjusting back to a nonpregnant condition.

AFTER-BIRTH BLUES

I hated feeling run down, zapped of my zest for life. I wanted to get on with a full routine and my body rebelled. Every fiber kept screaming, "Slow down!" But I didn't want to.

I was depressed by my lack of energy. A couple of weeks after delivery I read some helpful material written by Dr. William Sears. He talked about postpartum depression and the fact that fatigue is a large factor in the after-birth experience. Dr. Sears says:

At least fifty percent of all women giving birth in North American hospitals experience some degree of postpartum depression. Symptoms include the following: lack of energy, episodes of crying, anxiety, fear, headaches, worry about physical appearance and attractiveness, mild insomnia, confusion, and a negative attitude towards the husband. These feelings are generally thought to be caused by the rapid drop in the level of maternal hormones following childbirth.[1]

It helped to know I wasn't alone in my fatigue, and it was encouraging to realize that there was a physiological reason for my lack of energy. In other words, it wasn't all in my head! Be encouraged—it's not all in your head!

RESUMING A SEXUAL RELATIONSHIP

The last question I asked Dr. Petersen before leaving the hospital was, "When can we have intercourse again?" He said, "Wait ten days to two weeks." This, I've found, is the typical waiting period. If other medical problems are involved, a doctor may instruct his patient to wait several weeks or even months until she has completely recovered.

After a miscarriage or stillbirth, it is sometimes difficult for a couple to talk about having intercourse. Karen put it this way: "It had been three weeks since the miscarriage and we still hadn't made love. I think both of us were afraid to bring up the subject. Sex was tied so much to our loss that it was too painful to think about it. After about six weeks we finally talked about our feelings. Steve said that for awhile, he was just too depressed to consider it. Then he was afraid to approach me about making love because he thought it might bring back all the bad memories."

During the weeks immediately following a loss it is important for the couple to express affection and to hold one another even though intercourse is not permitted. At a time when you both feel vulnerable and depressed, it's good to be generous with your affection. Renee shared these ideas: "We knew we couldn't have intercourse for two weeks but my needs to be held and kissed were still there. In fact, they were stronger than usual because of the emptiness I felt inside for our baby. To be held did more to comfort me than a thousand words at times."

Sometimes a grieving woman may interpret a husband's sexual advances as an intrusion, or as a violation against her right to grieve. Jack and Marilyn each shared their struggles: "I remember trying to comfort Marilyn and thinking that my affection would help. But she wouldn't respond. I tried to communicate my love for her through sexual expressions but it didn't help. I think it just made matters worse." Marilyn said, "It really bugged me that Jack kept wanting to make love. I kept thinking—why isn't he grieving? How can he think about sex when our baby is dead?"

A couple's sexual relationship is a very important part of marriage. The most critical thing to remember at a time like this is that it is an absolute necessity to be open and to talk about your feelings concerning sex. Explain your thoughts to one another. Talk out your fears and concerns and be patient with each other.

If you view your sexual relationship as an expression of intimacy and communication, you will find that your sex life will undoubtedly be enhanced after your loss. There is an added need for both of you to be loved and nurtured during your grief. Sexual expression is one way to meet that need.

Both fears related to another pregnancy and guilt can hinder your sexual relationship. If you are experiencing sexual difficulties, consider the following counsel:

• Realize that depression and a decreased sex drive go hand in hand. During the intensity of your grief it is normal not to desire sexual arousal. As time passes you will regain desire bit by bit.

• If you have fears about pregnancy, talk about them and write them down. Some of the fears you have might be alleviated by talking with your doctor. Call for an appointment and settle some of those hidden questions once and for all.

• If you want to wait awhile before trying to conceive again, use contraceptives for protection rather than total abstinence.

• Some couples feel guilty because miscarriage began shortly after they had intercourse. This is a form of false guilt. There is no scientific proof that intercourse causes miscarriage. So don't blame your loss on your sexual relations.

• Some people feel guilty for enjoying sex when "they should be grieving." This is not a healthy attitude. Why keep beating yourself for something that is over and in the past? Move on with life. It's okay to enjoy intimacy with your mate. Depriving yourself of the joys of sex won't solve anything, it won't bring your baby back . . . it will only complicate matters.

• Variety is the spice of life. Try providing yourselves with opportunities to enhance your sexual expressions. You might want to use a dim light or candles if you usually make love in the dark. Or try escaping for a weekend to a vacation spot of your choice. Use creativity to make things more interesting.

If you find it difficult to deal with this topic alone, don't hesitate to seek professional help from a pastor or counselor. There is no need for your sexual relationship to suffer. A trained counselor can help you over these hurdles and give you tools to strengthen your relationship.

Chapter Thirteen

Eating for Health

One morning about a week after I lost the baby, I wrote the following entry in my journal: "I've had a terrible time sleeping lately. The grandfather clock gonged at 2:00 A.M. and I realized I hadn't dozed a wink. The alarm went off at 7:00 A.M. John needed breakfast and I was supposed to be at work in fifty-five minutes. Begrudgingly, I slithered out of bed with bloodshot eyes. My instincts told me, 'Plug in the coffee pot.'

"Waiting for that first cup, I picked up a ladies' magazine on the kitchen table and read some inspiring words written by someone who had obviously not just lost a baby. It said, 'You can feel more energetic if you'll just think positively. Simply recite this prescribed formula: "It's a wonderful day! I'm so happy to be alive! Act enthusiastic and you'll be enthusiastic! Your PMA [Positive Mental Attitude] will guarantee a great day full of rest and wonder!" If this doesn't leave you with the feeling of a marathon high, then put on your favorite dress that is just "your color" and primp with the latest designs in makeup. Energy will ooze from your being.'"

There were several mornings I faced the mirror thinking, "Good Lord, Pam—you look awful! Quick—grab the Max Factor blush!" Thank God for make-up at times like that. My energy level was about as droopy as the bags under my eyes. I felt lousy. Sometimes I didn't know which end was up. I figured that must be normal since it had only been one week since the delivery.

Five weeks later my thoughts were, "I should be feeling much better. It's been over a month." No such luck. It was actually worse because I had expected to be back to normal by then, but I felt bloated and flabby. I was extremely tired and had heart palpitations every now and then. That scared me. I had always been healthy and energetic. Deep down I was convinced I would be this tired, this heavy, this weepy, and this confused the rest of my life. I felt out of control and I hated it.

My confusion and impatience with a drained energy level drove me back to the books. I wanted some answers. There had to be a quicker way to build my body back to full strength. I discovered that medical research has shown that one of the most physically vulnerable times for a woman is after pregnancy, especially after a difficult delivery where blood loss has been excessive. I'd like to share with you some of the self-helps that aided me in regaining my physical strength and health.

PLEASE PASS THE DOUGHNUTS AND ICE CREAM

"But I want to pig-out!" This popular cliché becomes a lifestyle for some women following a pregnancy loss. Carolyn told me, "Sweets and desserts were what I wanted most after I miscarried. If I had a half-gallon of chocolate chip ice cream all to myself, I was happy. I forgot about my baby. The ice cream tasted good and let me forget. Doughnuts did the same thing. One afternoon the kids and I polished off three dozen together. I wasn't really hungry...

it just gave me an escape."

This story is not uncommon. Oftentimes the grieving mother will try to cope with the stress of losing a child by reaching into the pantry or refrigerator. The food becomes an anesthetic for her pain. This is one form of coping, but not the healthiest or most beneficial in the long run. It actually compounds suffering more because it leads to further weight gain with its frustrations. More fat + more guilt = more misery.

NUTRITION GUIDELINES

I've been told by nutrition experts that "I am what I eat." With my enthusiasm and energy for life averaging about a three on a scale of one to ten, I wanted all the help I could get to rebuild my strength. I knew that with proper nutrition, I was more likely to be a candidate for optimal health.

In his book *Diets Don't Work,* Bob Schwartz cites some amazing statistics:

> Do you know how many people actually get the results they want by dieting? One out of every two hundred! The failure rate of diets and weight loss programs is 99.5 percent. Out of every two hundred people who go on a diet, only ten lose all the weight they set out to lose. And of those then, only one keeps it off for any reasonable length of time.[1]

Most professionals whole heartedy agree with Bob— *diets don't work.* Yet, hundreds of diet books are on the market. New fad diets come out each month, and people buy the new releases, even though they already have twenty-five other diet books that didn't work. There is a desperate longing in the hearts of many to find a quick method for weight control.

For some reason many women feel that the more restrictive or rigid they are with a diet, the more successful they'll be controlling their weight. However, the opposite is true. The more restrictive the diet, the more likely they are to go off it and fail.

If you are struggling with weight control you have to make a choice. *You have to choose whether you want to continue to fight against seeing a certain number of pounds on the bathroom scale or whether you want to learn to eat normally and experience long term weight control.*

If you choose to remain obsessed with weight loss, the destructive chain of food's grasp on your life will tighten. If you choose to channel your energy toward learning how to eat normally, several positive by-products will be yours: increased peace of mind, stabilized eating patterns and a chance to begin effective lasting weight control.

PLAN TO SUCCEED

Those who fail to plan, plan to fail! A daily planner is an inexpensive way to bring order to your daily food consumption. A spiral notebook is a good place to keep a running record of your nutrition plan. Papers don't get lost, and you'll be able to look back over previous days to see your progress.

When are your vulnerable times with food? If evenings are tough, perhaps you'll want to record your plans after dinner. "Evenings are hard for me," Tina admitted. "I'm busy at work and school all day and have no desire to overeat, but when I get home, I'm depressed about losing the baby and food relaxes me and brings consolation. At least I used to think it did. Actually I ended up with more anxiety, hating myself after eating so much. Now I plan my evening. Every morning I have a fifteen-minute break at work. That's my time to plan a strategy for the evening." Tina's list includes these activities.

Take a bubble bath and read one of my favorite magazines.

Watch TV with a project that will keep my hands busy, such as crafts, sewing, needlepoint, laundry, or ironing.

Write letters.

Clean closets, organize my desk, or redo files.

See a movie with friends.

Go shopping or browse in bookstores.

Exercise at the health spa or with an aerobic video.

Ask a friend to go out for coffee.

Listen to my relaxation tape or other favorite tapes.

Read a good book.

Ride my exercise bike during the evening news.

Take my dog for a leisurely walk in the park.

Pamper myself with a facial or manicure.

Maybe the break time at work is a trial for you because everyone else is having coffee and doughnuts. Try writing your battle plans during your break. You'll be amazed how uninteresting those doughnuts will become.

"It sure worked for me!" exclaimed Corin. "By eliminating those mid-morning doughnut breaks, I lost two pounds the first week!"

Kathy told me that her vulnerable time was driving to

and from work. She said, "I used to hit all of the fast-food restaurants in one area each trip. Now I have a specific plan for that weakness. Before I leave in the morning I eat a small but healthy breakfast. Then I tell myself, 'Your only goal for this next hour is to drive straight to work with no stops.' I leave the checkbook at home and take just enough change to buy a soda with my lunch. Then I pray on my way to work.

Weekends were distressing for Toni. "They used to be my bummer days," she explained. "Now they're fun. I reward myself on Saturday for all the binges I passed up during the week. I use my calculator to determine how much money I've saved through the week when I turned down a binge in the heat of temptation. Then I buy a new pair of earrings or something special for myself. Some times Marty and I will use the money to go to the movies or to buy records. This reward system really keeps me motivated through the week, and it gives me something fun to do on weekend."

Eating out with friends can challenge anyone trying to maintain healthy eating habits. But with proper planning, restaurant dining can be a healthy and enjoyable experience. The key principles to remember when eating out are:

Eat in moderation;

Eat in restaurants willing to prepare foods without added fat, salt, sauces, and gravies;

If you do not know what is in an item and how it is prepared—ask!

Your waiter-waitress should readily know how your food is prepared;

If on a calculated diet, remember to bring your meal plan so that substituting foods can be done at a glace;

Watch your portions. If too large, do not eat all that you have been served. Do ask for a "doggie bag";

Ask for low-fat dressings, low-fat milk, fresh fruits. More restaurants are carrying them;

Ask for dressings, sauces, margarine, or butter to be served on the side, so you can control the portion;

Avoid foods in which calorie, fat, or sodium content cannot be reasonably estimated;

Most foods in restaurants are prepared with salt, so don't use extra at the table.[2]

Have healthy snackes available. Whatever time of day or night is your vulnerable time, you will be more likely to stick to healthy snacks if they are readily available. Health food stores and many grocery and variety stores carry an assortment of quick, easy snacks. Unbuttered microwavable popcorn is an excellent example of a quick, low-fat snack. Weight Watchers and other companies produce several packaged, ready-to-eat snacks, from dried fruits to mini rice cakes to unsalted pretzels. Of course, nothing beats a snack of fresh fruits or vegetables.

Arrange your schedule to avoid being overwhelmed. After Marian tried planning her day, she told me about her frustration: "In the morning I get up and feel overwhelmed with everything that needs to be done. I panic, which leads me to the refrigerator. Now I have a plan of action and turn my mornings into an opportunity to win. I set my alarm fifteen minutes earlier and sit at the kitchen table with a cup of coffee and my daily planner. On the left side of the page

I write down the things that need to be done in order of priority. Then on the right I try to plan exactly what jobs I'll do for the day and what can be left for another day. Writing out a planned list takes away the confusion in doing my responsibilities. As I get each job done, I take a big red marker and cross another accomplishment off the list. I gain great satisfaction from seeing my progress through the day."

Yes, it does take time and energy to plan. But the benefits of normal eating are worth it. Set a goal to invest yourself in planning to succeed. Remember, if you aim at nothing, you'll be sure to hit it! Normal eating habits won't happen overnight, but as you plan, set goals, and take it one day at a time, you will see success.

Helpful Hints for Weight Control

As you work with your plans for freedom, try some methods advocated by many weight control programs. New behaviors are learned and developed. They don't happen automatically, and normal eating patterns will come easier if you utilize some of the following tips:

Set Short-range goals and force yourself to think in the here and now. Today is the only day you need to handle, now. You don't have to handle everything all at once. Don't look at the huge mountain of the overall goal. Focus on the one step that needs to be taken at the present moment. Instead of being overwhelmed with thoughts of the entire week, concentrate on making it through the next hour or the next meal.

Reward yourself when you stick to your battle plan. Marian came up with a great reward system. She earned a credit for every meal she stuck to her battle plan. As the credits accumulated, she treated herself with rewards. Here are some of her ideas: renting a video; exercising an extra morning at the athletic club with the kids in the nursery; spending a

day at the beach with a friend; signing up for an oil paint-
ing class; buying a new accessory for her wardrobe.

Try not to use food as a reward. Some people use food
such as candy bars or doughnuts as a present for accom-
plishing a difficult task. While you are trying to learn to eat
normally, substitute other rewards, like a bubble bath or a
favorite magazine or a new bottle of nail polish, in place of
food.

Remove binge foods from your house, particularly trigger
foods. You can't eat what you don't have.

If family members want sweets, and you know it would
upset the household to deprive them of desserts, *keep these
items out of sight* or in containers that are out of easy reach.

Don't go grocery shopping while you're hungry. Write out
your shopping list according to your battle plans, and shop
on a full stomach. You will be more likely to stay away from
high-calorie "extras."

All of these ideas serve one purpose: they make it hard
for you to fudge on your battle plans. Don't allow yourself
to be surrounded by stimuli that will pull out the worst in
you. Instead, surround yourself with stimuli that will help
your toward your goals."

When I was confronted with the suggestions offered by
nutrition experts, I decided I'd give them a try. After all...I
didn't have anything to lose (aside from some excess bag-
gage), and the Lord knows how I needed more bounce in
my step! I did have to invest some extra thought into meal
planning, but the pay-offs were worth it. My energy and
strength began to increase and I felt better about myself and
about life in general.

God did a marvelous job creating the human body. He
designed us with extreme intricacies that intertwine at a
physical, mental, emotional, and spiritual level. I'll never
cease to be amazed at the extensive and effective healing
capacity God has built into our systems. After a pregnancy
loss, your body is weakened and vulnerable. The best thing

you can do right now is to work with your body and with God in the healing process. Even while eating out, try to choose those foods that will work for you and not against you. Remember, it's your God-given privilege to work with Him on rebuilding you!

Chapter Fourteen

Mood Swings and Exercise

I know . . . you've heard it all before. If you're like a lot of women, you've probably been razzle-dazzled by 101 different exercise experts on the front lines of the body-conditioning craze. Perhaps you're thinking, "That's great for Jane Fonda, Richard Simmons, and Marie Chapian, but that's not where I'm at. I always start out with great intentions to exercise regularly. But then after a few weeks I can't find my tennis shoes and my leotards have runs in them."

Or maybe your response takes on a different tune that rings something like this: "I never have liked to exercise. Besides, I don't have time. I'm up at 6:00 A.M. and off to work by 7:00 A.M. By the time I get home from work, I'm too exhausted to do anything except eat dinner and get the house in order. It just doesn't fit into my schedule."

Those are the ways a lot of us look at exercise. We either say, "Oh, what's the use—I've already tried and failed," or "I don't have the time or the energy to invest in it," or "I've never cared much for exercise and have been fine without it, so why start now?"

An exercise program can be beneficial after a loss because it helps elevate moods and stabilize mood swings. God knows how profound those emotional roller coaster rides can be!

There were many days after I delivered when my moods were anything but stable. I remember dragging myself down to the athletic club on lunch hours to swim. I'd enter the club depressed and irritable, wishing I didn't have to face the rest of the day. But after swimming a hard and fast mile, things were better. I had more energy, my blues weren't as black, and I was more optimistic about the hours ahead.

Psychological and medical researchers continue to affirm the fact that exercise affects moods in a positive way. C.H. Folkins showed in one study that psychological fitness is a function of physical fitness. He found that improvement in individuals on psychological measures of anxiety, depression, self-confidence, adjustment, work efficiency, and sleep behavior was directly related to physical fitness improvements. R.S. Brown found that anger, hostility, fatigue, tension, and anxiety were significantly lowered in people who jogged. Positive feelings of cheerfulness, energy, and activity were also significantly increased. Many other studies could be added to these which have documented the positive effects of exercise on moods. Some doctors are now prescribing regular exercise programs for depressed patients and finding excellent results.[1]

One explanation for the mood elevations that occur during exercise is that as the body exerts energy in a work-out, endorphines are released in the brain. These endorphines are the body's natural tranquilizers and antidepressants. And believe me—they are a whole lot cheaper than behind-the-counter drugs. Good physical exercise will not only leave you feeling relaxed and refreshed, but it will also

help your outlook on life. A little huffing, puffing, and per-
spiration really can help chase the postpartum blues away.

GETTING STARTED

"I'll start next week," is a well-intentioned promise.
There's one problem with it. Next week turns into next
month and before you know it, you're back to making
another one of those ridiculous New Year's resolutions. A
better thing to say would be, "I'll start today—even if I only
exercise ten minutes, it's still a start!" Then back that state-
ment up with, "God...help me get started...help me stick
with it and not give up." Then *do* it.

Before you begin to huff and puff and glow (another
word for sweat), it's best to decide on the type of exercise
you want to do and are capable of doing after your pregnancy loss. Some doctors prefer that you don't exercise for
several weeks following a miscarriage or stillbirth because
of the possibility of hemorrhaging. My doctor instructed me
not to swim for a few weeks after delivery due to the possibility of infection. He wanted to give the cervix time to completely heal before I plunged into a chlorinated pool. Please
follow your doctor's instructions. You want exercise to
work for you and not against you. But once permission is
given, don't hesitate to begin.

Studies have shown that the greatest fitness improvements are made when the heart is stressed at 70 to 80 percent of its maximum potential. Improved fitness comes
from lengthening the exercise, not by trying to do more
work in the same amount of time. So don't make the mistake of trying to go out and do it all in one day. Over exercise is as bad as no exercise. Start slow and gradually build
up to the fitness you desire.

WHAT'S BEST FOR YOU?

It's frustrating. Go to the exercise and fitness section in your local bookstore and you'll find experts telling you to do everything from running the stairs in your house twenty times a day to joining an elite gym for weight training seven days a week. What's a person to do?

The nice thing about exercise is that it works best for you when you choose a routine that is suited to you and is something you enjoy. I have many friends who run five to ten miles a day. They look great and feel great. But jogging isn't for me. It bothers my back and I feel worse after three miles than I did when I started. The main thing to remember is that you're exercising to strengthen your body, to become more fit, and to help your moods. Most people agree that aerobic exercises are unquestionably the most efficient.

One of my friends who experienced a stillbirth had a difficult time going to her spa the month following delivery. She had exercised regularly all through pregnancy. But it was just too hard for her to face people and their questions and comments regarding her loss. She decided to exercise in other ways. Instead of going to the aerobic dance classes, she and her husband set aside some time each day to take a brisk walk around the blocks in their neighborhood. When that wasn't convenient because of conflicting schedules or needs of her children, she spent twenty minutes jumping rope.

There are a lot of self-help tools on the market that can make aerobic exercise more convenient for you. If you have other small children at home and find it hard to get out of the house for exercise, don't lose heart. You can exercise aerobically in your own home. To make it more fun, you might want to invest in one of the latest videos. Then squeeze your aerobic routine into your day at your convenience. Your local Christian bookstore can give you a list of the latest videos available.

If you have the option of visiting a spa on a regular basis, take advantage of that option. Try to set a time when you can work out on a regular basis and then begin to establish a new habit in your lifestyle. Habits are easily formed. Exercise would be a good habit to incorporate now to help you cope with your stress and to strengthen your body for the possibility of future family plans.

It's important to remember that you're the best judge of what your body can handle right now. You may find at the start that you have very little energy or endurance. Most women don't after a pregnancy! In fact, current research says it takes a woman's body at least one year to fully recuperate from a pregnancy. So pace yourself according to your physical needs. Realize the limitations you have now are justifiable. Gradually you will feel stronger and have more bounce in your step. It just takes time.

Chapter Fifteen

The Trauma of a Tubal Pregnancy

I t all started with a simple pain in my lower left abdomen." Suzanne and I were sitting in my living room, and she was recalling for me the details of her last pregnancy. I'll let her tell her story:

"Being the busy mother of five children, with little time for interruptions of this sort, I chose to ignore it. But as the days passed, the pain intensified and started robbing me of sleep. Since Jim is a family practice physician, I try to shield him from my aches and pains so that when he comes home, he's off duty as much as possible. But this couldn't wait. In the middle of the night I casually mentioned my discomfort. After examining me, he asked me to see my gynecologist in the morning. The concern and urgency in his voice puzzled me.

"I complied, shuffled the kids off to the baby sitter first thing in the morning and headed straight to Dr. Raghu's office. Jim called ahead to notify them I was coming. I felt grateful that they squeezed me in because an hour later Dr.

Raghu was leaving for a conference. He examined me and within minutes a pregnancy test revealed that I was pregnant. But I could tell something was wrong. The doctor wasn't his usual chipper self, and he somberly told me he wanted to run some more tests.

"'More tests'", I thought. 'This never happened when I found out I was pregnant with my other five. What's going on?'" Confusion dominated my thoughts and I kicked into automatic pilot, following the medical staff's instructions to move into the ultrasound room. I tried to read their faces for some kind of clue as to what was going on. The ultrasound screen confirmed the doctor's suspicions. The images on the monitor revealed a lot of blood and no baby. After extracting fluid from behind the uterus with a needle, Dr. Raghu gently said, 'Suzanne, this test indicates there is a possibility that you have had a tubal pregnancy, and one of your fallopian tubes has ruptured.'

"Within minutes we were in Dr. Raghu's office calling my husband. Dr. Raghu used a lot of medical jargon when he talked to Jim, but what I understood from the conversation was that we were faced with surgery, risks, a possible rupture, and the removal of a fallopian tube—IMMEDIATELY. Reality set in. I wasn't going to bring this baby home, and Dr. Raghu wasn't going to his conference.

"Jim finally arrived. I recall feeling somewhat guilty because he had to cancel his patients for the day. Nothing could have been farther from his mind. He scrubbed and joined me in the operating room. I laid on the table amazed that only a few hours before I hadn't even known I was pregnant. I had never felt this baby move. I had never dreamed dreams for this child. I had never even "tried" to have it. Now this. The truth is, the full impact of what was happening to me had not sunk in yet.

"After the procedure I opened my eyes to another familiar place. I knew I was in the recovery room. But why? Oh yes, the tubal pregnancy. Before I could fully focus, a wave of sadness washed over me and the tears poured out long and hard. Jim and the nurse attended to me immediately, trying to determine if I was in pain. But the pain I was feeling was beyond their ability to medicate. It went much deeper than the little incision on my stomach. It was a wounded heart that only God and time could heal.

"Jim told me how grateful he was that God had saved my life. He saw the ruptured fallopian tube and noticed that the bleeding had stopped on its own. Other cases in his medical background had shown him that excessive bleeding can lead to death.

"His words surprised me. I had had no idea I was in such danger. The slight physical pain leading up to the surgery seemed insignificant to me. All kinds of questions darted back and forth in mind. I realized I knew very little about my body's reproductive organs."

WHAT HAPPENED TO MY BODY?

Like most women who suffer a tubal pregnancy, Suzanne had no time to prepare. Caught off guard by the whole ordeal, she was left to wrestle the many questions which often follow such medical procedures. In the days following her hospital stay, Suzanne was determined to learn all she could about her body and about tubal pregnancies. Focusing on the facts kept some of her confusion at bay and quieted her fears. I hope the basic information about tubal pregnancy that follows will do the same for you.

What is a tubal (ectopic) pregnancy? It is a pregnancy that develops outside the uterus, commonly in the fallopian tube, but sometimes in the ovary or, rarely, in the abdominal cavity or cervix. Ninety-five percent of ectopic pregnancies develop in the fallopian tube.[1]

It can be pictured in this way:

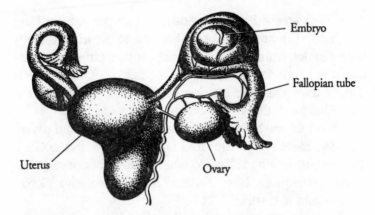

How common are ectopic pregnancies? About one in every fifty pregnancies is ectopic. In the past twenty years the number of diagnosed ectopics has quadrupled, partly due to the continuing epidemic of tube-damaging, sexually transmitted infections and also because of better diagnostic methods.[2]

No single cause of ectopic pregnancy has been identified, but a number of factors place women at high risk. Ectopic pregnancies are more common if there is some congenital abnormality of the fallopian tubes, if the pelvic area has been previously operated on or infected, if the woman has used an IUD for birth control, and had previous ectopic pregnancies.[3] They are also more likely if the woman has been taking the progesterone-only birth control pill or has undergone a failed sterilization, especially if the fallopian tubes have been cauterized.[4] Hormones seem to play a role, too. An ovum's normal rate of transport through the tube requires ample hormonal stimulation; if stimulation is reduced, the embryo's progress slows and occasionally halts.[5]

A history of pelvic inflammatory disease is the most common predictor; it's found in one of every four women who develop an ectopic pregnancy.[6] Age, race, and economic status also have an influence. Women between thirty-five and forty-four and black teenagers are at greater risk, followed closely by minority and poor women of all ages.[7]

Are tubal pregnancies dangerous to the mother? Yes, they can be life-threatening. Ten percent of deaths resulting from pregnancy complications are related to a tubal pregnancy. Ectopic pregnancy is the single leading cause of maternal death in the United States.[8]

Is there anything a woman can do to prevent a tubal pregnancy from occurring? If a woman follows the Biblical injunctions to limit sexual relations to the marriage relationship, she diminishes the chances of contracting a sexually transmitted disease which can damage the fallopian tubes. However, many women who have suffered tubal pregnancies did follow these guidelines and did not previously have a sexually transmitted disease.   When the reproductive organs appear to be in good condition, it is likely that the normal reproductive process simply malfunctioned and the egg just got stuck in the tube on it's way down to the uterus. In cases like this there is nothing the woman could have done to prevent the tubal pregnancy.

What kinds of complications arise as a result of tubal pregnancies? In severe cases the mother can go into shock due to extreme blood loss, particularly if the fallopian tube ruptures. In some cases the mother's life is lost.

What are the symptoms of a tubal pregnancy? Lower abdominal pain that is usually cramped and one-sided, slight vaginal bleeding, and a history of at least one missed period are the classic triad of symptoms of ectopic pregnancy. But not all women have these symptoms.   One woman in ten feels no pain until rupture is imminent, usually after the third month. One in four experiences abdominal pain but continue to menstruate. Others complain of vague or diffuse pain or mistake the discomfort for menstrual cramps. Because of the varied presentation, misdiagnosis of everything from endometriosis to an ovarian cyst to impending miscarriage is common.[9]

What is the general form of treatment for an ectopic pregnancy? Years ago ectopic pregnancy almost always meant major surgery and the removal of the tube. Today the trend is to use less invasive treatment which preserves the tube and the woman's fertility whenever possible. Success depends on early diagnosis. The current methods of treatment are laparotomy, laparoscopy, and methotrexate.[10]

Laparotomy. Historically this was the standard treatment for ectopic pregnancies. It is the most invasive of all procedures. This surgery is used when a woman's tube ruptures and when it is imperative that bleeding be stopped. The doctor will attempt to repair the tube using microsurgery, but if the tube cannot be preserved, it will be removed. Patients usually stay in the hospital for several days post-op.

Laparoscopy. When a laparoscopy is performed the patient is usually placed under general anesthesia. Then laser surgery or microsurgery can be used to remove the fetus and repair the tube. Barring no complications, the woman can go home within twenty-four hours after the surgery.

Methotrexate. This drug, generally used for cancer chemotherapy, is given to dissolve an early ectopic pregnancy when there is no sign of blood leakage. Because the drug has side effects such as nausea, depression of bone marrow, and suppression of the immune response system, it is not used lightly or routinely. During surgery, if it does not appear that all the placental tissue was able to be removed from the tube, a doctor may chose to inject a small amount of methotrexate into the tube to kill off any remaining tissue. This prevents the placental tissue from replicating and growing beyond the tube's limits which could lead to a tubal rupture, hemorrhaging, and another surgery.

Doctors can determine the success of the procedure with ultrasound tests and by checking HCG levels in the blood. HCG levels are checked for a downward trend each week for six weeks following surgery. If the HCG levels do not return to normal, a physician may discuss the option of the patient taking oral methotrexate to kill off the final placental tissue left in the tube.[11]

Is it possible to have other children following a tubal pregnancy? Yes. This is true even when one of the tubes have been removed, although the chances of conception are somewhat reduced. Of those who do conceive, it is estimated they have an 85 percent chance of having a normal intrauterine pregnancy.[12] A woman who has had a previous ectopic pregnancy should seek medical care early in any subsequent pregnancy so that the doctor can determine the location of the fetus.[13]

THE STRUGGLES AFTER SURGERY

A large part of the emotional struggle following a tubal pregnancy comes from not being able to control the circumstances or the results on our bodies. Tamara, who suffered a miscarriage several years prior to a tubal pregnancy put it this way: "I think I struggled more after the tubal pregnancy than after my miscarriage because of the way the tubal pregnancy affected my body. I felt like I was half a woman after the surgery. The rupture created such extensive damage that the doctor had to remove my left tube and ovary.

"And instead of having a nice flat tummy when the whole ordeal was over, I was left with a pot belly where the incisions had been made."

My friend, Bonnie, also struggled with physical challenges after her surgery: "I didn't like having a scar. We had only been married a year and the surgery was very invasive, leaving a permanent reminder of the whole ordeal. Besides that it was a long road getting back in shape. But since that particular surgery, I have had several other surgeries which have left many scars on my legs. I guess through the years I have grown to accept the scars as part of me.

"In this life there are going to be things I don't like about my body, but I don't want to give those things more attention that they are worth. My body is simply a shell or a house for the Holy Spirit and me to live in. I try to keep my focus on the bigger picture. God has plans and intentions for me that will never be limited by the scars on my belly or legs. I want my zoom lens to be focused on what God is doing in my life rather than on the flaws of my body."

In some cases when the mother's life is dangerously at risk, much of the attention is focused on saving the woman's life and the loss of the baby is minimized or completely disregarded. When Connie was recovering from surgery, she couldn't understand why her visitors didn't acknowledge the loss of the pregnancy. Her doctor said, "We saved your life," but he never showed sympathy about the pregnancy ending. "Everything went well," is supposed to be good news coming from a doctor. But, often it leaves the woman who has lost the pregnancy upset.

Miriam told me, "I had just found out I was pregnant, with a home pregnancy test three weeks earlier. I dreamed about our baby, how I would decorate the nursery, what we would name him or her, and how the baby would look. The next thing I know my doctor tells me I have to have surgery. I wasn't sick. I wasn't in pain. I just had some light spotting. When the surgery was over, no one talked to me about our baby, they just told me I was lucky because they had saved my tube."

If you have suffered a tubal pregnancy, you have experienced both a physical assault and an emotional shock. This can threaten your overall sense of well-being. Laura said it well: "I feel so vulnerable now. The tubal pregnancy could have taken my life, and who is to say it won't happen again. I don't know if we'll ever be able to have a baby." Clearly, hope for a future pregnancy is clouded by the fear of another ectopic pregnancy or infertility.

Three emotions seem to be freshly on the surface of women who have had a tubal pregnancy: guilt, anger, and fear. Guilt can come from wondering if they may have done something to cause the tubal pregnancy, especially if sexual activity in earlier years had lead to pelvic inflammatory infections. Although an earlier abortion is unlikely to have contributed to the ectopic pregnancy, it may emerge now as a source of guilt. There is the realization that a choice was made to terminate a pregnancy in the past, not knowing it might be very difficult to have a child later on in life. This intensifies grief.

Anger often comes from the feeling of being "ripped off," of not being able to bring home a baby and for having to leave a part of their reproductive system in the operating room. Others feel angry because people surrounding the family minimized the pregnancy loss or anger with God for allowing it to happen or anger with their husbands for not showing more emotion or anger at themselves for not having a body that "worked right." And the list continues.

Anger and fear are often bosom buddies. The information Bonnie was given after her tubal pregnancy in 1975 evoked a fear that was hard to shake. At the time she was working to put her husband Greg through medical school and the tubal pregnancy came as a complete surprise: "I woke up that morning feeling ill, bloated, and rather cramped from what I thought was my menstrual period. After a few hours at work I started feeling dizzy. Greg suggested I see my doctor. Following an exam the doctor decided to remove the IUD I had been using for birth control and prescribed heavy doses of antibiotics. I went home and went to bed.

"By 2:00 P.M. unbeknownst to me, I had bled so much internally that my chest cavity had filled with blood, mak-

ing it difficult for me to breath. Greg took me in to Dr.
Neilson, who rushed me immediately into emergency after
I passed out on his examining room floor. When they
opened me up, they realized that one on my fallopian tubes
had ruptured and I had lost 1000 ccs of blood. It was clear to
Greg that I had come very close to death and he was deeply
thankful to God and to the medical community for sparing
my life.

"It all happened so fast. I didn't even know I was pregnant, much less that my life was in danger. Since I wasn't
aware of the pregnancy, and Greg and I were not wanting to
start a family until he finished medical school, I really didn't
feel the grief many experience after losing a baby. I was just
grateful to be alive. However, when the doctor told me after
the surgery that I might not be able to have children in the
future, that's when the grief hit me. That night I was recovering in my room on the labor and delivery ward, surrounded by mothers and families who were enjoying their
newborn babies. I realized those families had something I
didn't have, and may never have. Their excitement magnified my loss. It scared me to think my chances for having
children had been compromised."

Clearly, a tubal pregnancy is traumatic, and puts the
mother and family into a state of crisis. The emotional aftermath is a long slow struggle, like it is for those who have
suffered miscarriage or stillbirth. Many painful questions
and issues intrude into daily thoughts. And in most cases
there are many more questions than there are answers.

I've written this chapter primarily to give you a brief
overview of some of the common challenges and questions
women face when they suffer a tubal pregnancy. More
information can be gleaned from medical books and other
resources found in your public library. If you have lost a
baby, I encourage you to take good care of yourself. Seek
out information that will give you added perspective.
Check into various support organizations where you can

meet others who have gone through similar experiences. Resolve and Compassionate Friends are two organizations that are interested in helping those who have lost babies. They have chapters in many communities as well as publications available to the public. Above all else, please give yourself permission to feel the feelings as they come. It's okay not to feel okay for awhile.

Chapter Sixteen

New Beginnings

I still remember the first evening we talked about starting a family. We were so excited. We both burst out laughing about the idea of a baby crawling around the living room carpet. It had been six years since we walked the marriage aisle; we were ready to have children. With anticipation in our hearts and high hopes for a quick conception, we began a new chapter in our lives. Two and a half months later the pregnancy test came back positive.

It is now one year since that first conception occurred. Everything was progressing beautifully until the baby began its fifth month of growth . . . you know the rest of the story.

Several months have passed since we lost our baby. We have spent that time recuperating emotionally and physically from the jolt we suffered. We are now again at a place of new beginnings. The thermometer is once again on the bedside table, with all contraception set aside. What's it like starting again? Very different. The full blown excitement has been replaced with ambivalence. High hopes are intertwined with fear and apprehension of what a new pregnancy will bring. These vacillating emotions are generally not the exception but the rule among many couples who decide to try to conceive again.

PLANNING TOWARD ANOTHER PREGNANCY

During my post-operative exam I remember asking Dr. Petersen, "When is it okay to get pregnant again?" He encouraged me to wait until I had a normal menstrual cycle. While talking with other women, I found that doctors vary in their advice. There is no answer applicable to every woman. From a strictly physical standpoint some doctors suggest that a woman wait until she has had two normal menstrual periods before trying to get pregnant again. This time allows the body to heal and recuperate in preparation for another pregnancy. However, a woman must also consider her emotional well being and the impact that another pregnancy will make on family relationships.

Some couples eagerly pursue pregnancy immediately after a loss. Joanie said, "I hated not being pregnant. Once I got home from the hospital we started working on conceiving again. I hadn't even completed one full menstrual cycle when the pregnancy tests came back positive. It was the best thing that could have happened to us. It helped us forget the past and look forward to the future."

Other couples experience different feelings and have no desire to begin another pregnancy for many months or even years. Patsy shared her feelings, saying, "I don't want to get pregnant again for a long time. I want to forget everything about the stillbirth and pursue a career. Steven doesn't seem to be in disagreement. He said, 'Whatever you can handle is fine with me.'"

When considering the timing of another pregnancy, remember what is best for one couple could be detrimental to another. There is no set schedule that will suit every family. You and your mate are the experts when it comes to making this decision because you know better than anyone else how you are feeling physically and emotionally. You know best what you can and can't handle at this particular time in your life.

POSTLOSS PREGNANCY

Often the stress involved with a transition in life can be buffered if you have some idea of what to expect after the change. If and when you decide to plan another pregnancy there are some challenges you may face which are common to women who have suffered a loss. Being aware of these challenges can help you have realistic expectations concerning postloss pregnancy.

Challenge #1: Negative pregnancy tests. "We waited three months after I miscarried our second baby to try to conceive again. I felt positive and had hope for the days ahead. One month, two months, six months went by and there was still no sign of pregnancy. I'd get my hopes up when my menstrual period was overdue only to be let down a day later. I hated all the ups and downs. I lived from one menstrual period to the next, praying to God that it wouldn't come each month. I got to the point where I avoided talking to Martin about it because I hated seeing him disappointed every month, too. There was one month where my period was two weeks late and I thought for sure I was pregnant. I was even having headaches like I had during my first pregnancy. But the test results came back negative. Finally, after a year of trying, we conceived another baby. But during the twelve months in between we experienced very real disappointments. "

Many other couples can identify with Martin and Linda's experience. It isn't easy to face the monthly physical signs which announce that there has been no conception. For the couple who experienced immediate pregnancy in the past, a delay can be exasperating. Questions dart through the mind such as, "What is the matter with us? What are we doing wrong? Are we infertile?"

When you're faced with disappointments and doubts like these it helps to reexamine your expectations. It is unrealistic for all couples to expect to conceive quickly. Statistics prove this point. Research has shown that 60 percent of those couples trying to conceive are successful by the sixth month. Another 30 percent go on to conceive within the course of a year.[1] To expect immediate conception places inordinate demands on yourself and sets you up for disappointment. A more relaxed approach would stabilize the ups and downs. It might help to say something like this: "I hope I'm pregnant this month (that's honest) but if I'm not, it won't be the end of the world for me (that's realistic). We'll just have fun enjoying each other and see what happens." This will help alleviate the pressurized anxieties within and lighten your burden.

Challenge #2: Positive pregnancy tests and the nine months ahead. "I remember the day when David walked in the kitchen to report the doctor's findings. The pregnancy test was positive. We had done it! It was true! I was elated! Then it hit...an incredible fear crept in. All of my insides screamed, 'Oh God—will it happen again?' Those fears diminished only after I held little Amy in my arms nine months later. I hated myself for my lack of faith during the pregnancy. This was our third try. After two miscarriages I had intense doubts about whether or not we would ever bring a baby home with us. I'd think, 'God wouldn't let this happen again' but then a second later my thoughts were, 'but what if my body betrays me again?' The mental battles encompassed me.

"Months into my pregnancy I kept looking for evidence that I was pregnant. I'd wake up in the morning and make sure that my breasts were still sore and tender. If I was constipated I rejoiced! To me that meant that the baby was still okay because during my past two pregnancies I had experienced constipation up to the baby's death in the womb. Just before our losses the constipation changed to diarrhea (probably due to the hormone fluctuations in my body). Loose stools brought on extreme fear."

As Donna indicates, pregnancy does not necessarily bring release from frustrations. Rather, it is often a springboard for a new stream of fears and questions for the couple who have lost a baby.

Some couples are hesitant about preparing a nursery or buying things for the baby. They think, "If we fix everything up and then lose this one, too, we couldn't bear coming home and putting everything in the attic again." When friends offer to host baby showers the offer is refused. Even though the couple realizes that their friends are attempting to help them get excited, the fear that something may go wrong is too strong.

In talking with me, Donna elaborated on the fears she experienced. "During the entire nine months I lived from one doctor's appointment to the next. I'd never been more dependent on another person in all my life. He gave me constant reassurance in ways I needed. I depended on hearing him say, 'Everything is going well.' I looked for confidence from his reassuring eyes."

"My perception of life was drastically different during this pregnancy. I magnified every little thing that went wrong. It got to the point where I needed David to go to the doctor's appointments with me. During one appointment the doctor listened to the baby's heartbeat and said, 'It sounds pretty good.' 'Pretty good,' I thought. 'Wait a minute...pretty good isn't good enough. Something must be wrong...the baby isn't growing right...this one is going to die, too.' I blew one comment, which in reality meant that the baby was fine, completely out of proportion. David helped me achieve balance in this. His objectivity helped me to look at things in a more levelheaded fashion."

Although irrational, Donna's fears were very real. Relief and encouragement came when she quoted scripture and focused on God's Word rather than on her fears.

Challenge #3: After-birth anxieties. Some parents suffer particular anxieties even after a successful birth. If there has been a previous stillbirth much of the hospital experiences during the following birth evoke emotional flashbacks. Some find it difficult to believe that everything really is all right and that a healthy baby really will be going home with them. Janis put it this way: "They brought little Daniel in to me. I had so many mixed feelings all at once. I was so proud and happy to have him in my arms. But part of me kept reminiscing over Tiffany's stillbirth and the experience of holding her while knowing I couldn't take her home with me. I wanted to laugh and cry all at the same time. I had fears about Daniel's health. The doctor told me he couldn't be a more healthy nine-pound baby, but I still had fears that this baby would be snatched from us like the last one.

"The first few months at home with him were very difficult for me. I was afraid to let him out of my sight and I wanted to hold him all the time and hated to even leave the room for fear something might happen. Gradually the fears went away, but when they were there, they were very real."

FEARS ARE NORMAL

Many women have experienced these fears and anxieties during pregnancies following a loss. If you are having some of these feelings, be encouraged! You're normal! It would be abnormal not to have some degree of apprehension after living through the grief of a previous loss.

Fear is a challenging emotion to handle. It can paralyze. However, there are some steps that you can take to help reduce the intensity of fears and to protect yourself against being incapacitated by those feelings.

It helps to understand that when you were fearful, you were usually preoccupied with what you imagine could happen to someone or something. You may be preoccupied with imagining another loss, or imagining complications in a present or future pregnancy. The more you dwell on what might happen, the more fearful you become. The more fearful you feel, the more you concentrate on what may happen. It's a vicious circle that leaves a person feeling sapped of energy.

What can you do? It helps to be aware that fears are directly related to the imagination. If you take personal responsibility to discipline your imagination and your thought life, it can help you gain control over the feelings of fear. By choosing not to think and dwell on what might happen, you break the upward spiral of fearful feelings. Then you can channel your thoughts in a more healthy direction.

Donna's story gives an example of how to do this. When the irrational fears came she willfully chose not to focus on them and not to let her imaginations run wild. Instead, she quoted the scripture that encouraged her and channeled her thoughts in that direction. This helped to disarm the fears that had previously paralyzed her normal functioning ability.

It also helps to honestly and realistically appraise each situation we face. By facing reality we are better able to handle our feelings. It's easy to over generalize when we are fearful. For instance, you may be thinking, "I've had two miscarriages and I'll probably lose this pregnancy, too." This is an over generalization. Your two past pregnancies were separate and unique situations, different from your present pregnancy. It helps to assess your current situation based on the present facts. If you feel extremely overwhelmed by fear, ask your spouse or a friend to give you his objective viewpoint about matters. Like Donna, you'll benefit from the objectivity of others.

Once you have realistically faced your fears and the situations contributing to those fears, you have taken a big step toward emotional peace. It's easier to be lazy and fearful than to exert energy in order to do something that can improve your situation. But if there is something you can do to further alleviate those fears, then do it. For instance, Mary experienced some spotting during the fifth month of a pregnancy following a stillbirth. She could have roamed around the house engulfed in fear, wondering what was happening. This would have done nothing but intensify her anxieties. Instead she picked up the phone, called her doctor, and started asking questions. She found out some facts about spotting and learned that spotting doesn't necessarily mean a miscarriage is in process. By choosing to do what she could do in the situation, her fears were reduced. This is a characteristic of responsible living.

When we have taken all the steps possible to deal with our fears and with the surrounding circumstances, then it's best to "let go and let God." We need to put the matter in God's hands and realize there are things in life over which we have no control. Paul says it well in Philippians 4:6-7.

"Do not be anxious about anything, but in everything, by prayer and petition, with thanksgiving, present your requests to God. And the peace of God, which transcends all understanding, will guard your hearts and your minds in Christ Jesus."

Chapter Seventeen

The Bible Offers Hope and Comfort

W here do babies go when they die?" "I've always wondered what happened to that baby. Was it a person at just two months of growth? All we ever saw of its form was fragmented tissue."

"I never did figure out what happened to our baby. I just thought it probably ended up in 'nothingness' since it never lived past nine weeks of growth."

It is comforting to know that God provides answers to these questions in the Bible. His love for us is so great that He gives us understanding in the midst of our sorrows. He tells us that our miscarried or stillborn baby was in fact a very real person with a very alive soul and personality. Read these encouraging words from Psalm 139:1-18 (Living Bible):

"O Lord, you have examined my heart and know everything about me. You know when I sit or stand. When far away you know my every thought. You chart the path ahead of me, and tell me where to stop and rest. Every moment, you know where I am. You know what I am going to say before I even say it. You both precede and follow me, and place your hand of blessing on my head.

This is too glorious, too wonderful to believe! I can *never* be lost to your Spirit! I can *never* get away from my God! If I go up to heaven, you are there; if I go down to the place of the dead, you are there. If I ride the morning winds to the farthest oceans, even there your hand will guide me, your strength will support me. If I try to hide in the darkness, the night becomes light around me. For even darkness cannot hide from God; to you the night shines as bright as day. Darkness and light are both alike to you.

You made all the delicate, inner parts of my body, and knit them together in my mother's womb. Thank you for making me so wonderfully complex! It is amazing to think about. Your workmanship is marvelous—and how well I know it. You were there while I was being formed in utter seclusion! You saw me before I was born and scheduled each day of my life before I began to breathe. Every day was recorded in your Book!

How precious it is, Lord, to realize that you are thinking about me constantly! I can't even count how many times a day your thoughts turn towards me. And when I waken in the morning, you are still thinking of me!

Psalm 139 is an example of a beautiful prayer that David, the psalmist, wrote to God. In the words penned we find principles that apply not only to David, but also to every other person. When reading these scripture verses and viewing them in relation to a recent pregnancy loss; we find great comfort. Be encouraged by the truths set forth:

• God knows everything about you and your baby. "...you know everything about me" (v. 1).

• At every moment, God knows where you and your baby are. "Every moment you know where I am" (v. 2).

• God's hand of blessing is on you and your baby. "You place your hand of blessing on my head" (v. 5).

• Your baby has not gone into "nothingness," your baby is with God. "I can never be lost to your Spirit! I can *never* get away from my God!" (v. 7).

• Even though you feel alone and the blackness of death is all around you, God is as present with you and your baby now as He was when things were bright and cheery. "For even darkness cannot hide from God; to you the night shines as bright as day. Darkness and light are both alike to you" (v. 12).

• God was fully aware of the baby forming in your womb. "You made all the delicate, inner parts of my body, and knit them together in my mother's womb" (v. 13). "You were there while I was being formed in utter seclusion!" (v. 15).

• God was completely aware of the formation of your baby at every stage of life. "You saw me before I was born" (v. 16).

• God has a sovereign knowledge about each person's time for life and death. "You . . . scheduled

each day of my life before I began to breathe" (v. 16).
God knew all about the days of your baby in your
womb. Your baby is a very real person to God.

• God is constantly mindful of you in your suffering
and constantly mindful of your baby in His presence. "How
precious it is, Lord, to realize that you are thinking about me
constantly! I can't even count how many times a day your
thoughts turn towards me. And when I awake in the morning, you are still thinking of me" (vv. 17, 18).

Mary Hanes describes beautifully the truth of your
baby's being a person from the moment of conception. She
says:

> Only in recent years have scientists identified the
> DNA fibers woven into every human cell. We know
> now that from the moment of conception, every
> embryo has a DNA "blue print" which records
> exactly what that fetus is to become. Science has
> shown us "God's book." It is entirely sound to
> believe that when an embryo of even a few weeks is
> miscarried and lost to an earthly existence, God sim-
> ply develops that DNA "blueprint" in the heavenly
> kingdom. The Creator (whom Scripture even calls a
> Master Builder) simply completes the construction
> of what has already begun. To ask, "At what point
> does a human fetus receive a Spirit?" is to ask the
> wrong question. As Christians, we understand that
> a human being is spirit, soul and body; three ele-
> ments woven into one.[1]

Second Samuel 12:1-23 gives us further insight:

> On the seventh day the child died. David's ser-
> vants were afraid to tell him that the child was dead,

for they thought, "While the child was still living, we spoke to David but he would not listen to us. How can we tell him the child is dead? He may do something desperate."

David noticed that his servants were whispering among themselves and he realized the child was dead. "Is the child dead?" he asked.

"Yes," they replied, "he is dead."

Then David got up from the ground. After he had washed, put on lotions and changed his clothes, he went into the house of the LORD and worshiped. Then he went to his own house, and at his request they served him food, and he ate.

His servants asked him, "Why are you acting this way? While the child was alive you fasted and wept, but now that the child is dead, you get up and eat!"

He answered, "While the child was still alive, I fasted and wept. I thought, 'Who knows? The LORD may be gracious to me and let the child live.' But now that he is dead, why should I fast? Can I bring him back again? I will go to him, but he will not return to me."

From this story we glean the truth that when a baby dies, it goes to be with God. David said, "Can I bring him back again?" (implying "of course not"). And then he adds, "I shall go to him, but he will not return to me." David looked forward to the day when he would see his baby again.

This was one of the most comforting truths for us when our baby died. We couldn't bring the baby back to life, but we knew that one day we would see our baby in heaven. Second Corinthians 5:8 tells us that Paul preferred "rather to be absent from the body and to be at home with the Lord" (NASB). The instant our baby died it went to be with God.

There are other scriptures that give us more insight concerning life and personhood in the womb. Isaiah says, "Before I was born the LORD called me; from my birth he has made mention of my name" (Isaiah 49:1). God knew your baby in the womb!

Job said, ". . . why was I not hidden in the ground like a stillborn child, like an infant who never saw the light of day? There the wicked cease from turmoil, and there the weary are at rest" (Job 3:16, 17). In the midst of utter despair Job cries out to God, saying, "I wish I had been miscarried or stillborn! Then I wouldn't have to face the heartache and hassles of this world. Then I could have peace in my heart and be completely content." Your baby is experiencing that peace right now.

Ecclesiastes tells us that the miscarried or stillborn child has a better life in God's presence than do some individuals who live long lives: "A man may have a hundred children and live many years; yet no matter how long he lives, if he cannot enjoy his prosperity and does not receive proper burial, I say that a stillborn child is better off than he. It comes without meaning, it departs in darkness, and in darkness its name is shrouded. Though it never saw the sun or knew anything, it has more rest than does that man" (Ecclesiastes 6:3-5).

THE GRAVE IS NOT YOUR BABY'S FINAL DESTINATION

Do you ever think about heaven? I do. The Bible gives us some insight as to what to expect in heaven, but for the most part it will be so incredible that we're just going to have to see it to believe it! Jesus referred to heaven as "paradise" when talking to the dying thief on the cross next to Him. He said, "Today you will be with me in paradise" (Luke 23:43).

To me, paradise is the absence of pain or ugliness. With

that in mind, I rejoice over the fact that the quality of my baby's life at this very moment cannot be surpassed. My baby is experiencing more joy, more contentment, more happiness, and more satisfaction and love than this world could ever have given him. My baby will never experience the emotional heartache of suffering, or the physical pain of sickness and injury in this imperfect world. He is enjoying in totality the wonderful presence of God in a very perfect heaven. His death is the beginning of an eternal life in heaven. It does not end in the grave.

My baby understands wonderful experiences that I can only anticipate.

C. S. Lewis, in *The Last Battle*, fantasizes about what it will be like in heaven. A railway accident has just taken place and the children and parents in the story were killed. He describes the new beginning in these words:

> "There *was* a real railway accident.... Your father and mother and all of you are—as you used to call it in the Shadow-Lands—dead. The term is over: the holidays have begun. The dream is ended: this is the morning."
>
> And as He spoke He no longer looked to them like a lion; but the things that began to happen after that were so great and beautiful that I cannot write them. And for us this is the end of all the stories, and we can most truly say that they all lived happily ever after. *But for them, it was only the beginning of the real story. All their life* in this world and all their adventures in Narnia *had only been the cover and the title page:* now at last they were beginning Chapter One of the Great Story, which no one on earth has read: which goes on forever: in which every chapter is better than the one before.[2]

Yes, my baby's earthly life was very brief. The title page

of his life had only a few lines, but the chapters to follow will be full and marvelous. John and I have imagined and fantasized about what it must be like for our baby. During one of our conversations we talked about the possibility of our baby's sharing fellowship with John's dad. We had to laugh. On our second date, John invited me to his home for dinner. We had a great time around the table talking, and then out of nowhere John's dad, Ben, said, "I can just see little blond-haired, blue-eyed babies running all over this house!" This was only our second date! We couldn't believe our ears. I turned bright red and John kicked Ben under the table. John's dad had been the first to mention the desire to see us have children. As it turned out, Ben died in 1976. He was the first to see our baby and to enjoy the opportunity of getting to know him.

WHAT POSSIBLE GOOD CAN COME FROM DEATH?

A Christian couple I talked with said they received encouragement by thinking about the positive aspects of losing their baby. One idea they came up with was this: "We knew God doesn't make mistakes and that He has a perfect plan for each person's life. One reason He might not have allowed our daughter to experience life on earth may have been that He had a special job or mission for her in heaven. If God is preparing a place for us in heaven (John 14:2), it seems to me like there's a lot of action going on up there with work to be done and jobs to be handled. Perhaps our daughter is helping with that preparation."

Jim and Carol shared another positive occurrence that happened in the midst of their sorrow. Jim said, "Carol and I never knew we could have a personal relationship with God. We had gone to church for years and lived a good life helping people, but never knew we could be personally related to God. No one had ever told us that we could ask Jesus Christ into our hearts and acknowledge that He died on the cross for us as individuals. When our baby died, our neighbors came over and talked with us about God. They did a better job explaining death and God to us than did the minister at the funeral! We read several verses in the Bible together and that afternoon we realized that God loved us. We saw that God loved us and wanted to help us.

"That afternoon changed our lives. We prayed together and asked God to forgive us for all the sins of our past. We told Him that we accepted Christ's death on the cross for the payment of our sins. Then we asked Jesus Christ to be the Lord of our lives and to help us through this hard time and the rest of our lives. Our hearts have never been the same. God gave us hope at a time when no one else could. He strengthened us on the inside so that we could cope with our grief. Now Carol and I look forward to seeing Jenny in heaven and know without a doubt that we will one day be reunited."

Jesus Christ truly can give hope and comfort and strength beyond what words can express. Another story reaffirms this truth in a beautiful way. One week after suffering a miscarriage a friend of mine penned these words about her experience. Her perspective brought new awareness and understanding to pregnancy loss and offered encouragement to me. Renee wrote:

> I am so thankful to God for my special baby, even though he only lived eleven weeks after conception. Miscarriage was his return call by Jesus.
>
> I'll never be tempted to question the goodness of God in giving us a baby we never held. How could anyone be less than bursting with parental pride over a baby who brings you this much joy and expectation? I can't!
>
> When I made the announcement to Michael that our baby was coming he laughed first, then cried, and ended up doing both at the same time.

No other news on earth could have brought on this response, and the scene was repeated with grandparents. My baby's life was not long enough to have any pictures to carry in my billfold, but was long enough to fill my heart with wonderful memories.

I was never hurt by my child's rebellion, was never embarrassed by my child's actions, and I never had to discipline him. This was my child who brought me only joy all the days of his life. Thank you, God, for that kind of child; it was a gift only you could give.

Renee had beautiful insight even in the midst of her heartache. She had no anger toward God, only thanksgiving. Though her sorrow was very real, she chose to focus on the positive aspects of her loss. Philippians 4:8 says, "Whatever is true, whatever is noble, whatever is right, whatever is pure, whatever is lovely, whatever is admirable—if anything is excellent or praiseworthy—think about such things." We can learn from Renee's example.

IF GOD LOVES ME, WHY DID HE KILL MY BABY?

This is not an uncommon question and every couple who has lost a baby knows the agonizing experience of grappling with: "Why did God let my baby die?" Many look to God and shake an angry fist, saying, "You could have stopped this! Why did you take our baby away from us?"

The whole issue of pain, evil, and suffering is a difficult one to deal with, especially in the midst of depression. Because our grief stricken emotions often cloud and distort reality, it is hard to acknowledge that no one can be blamed for our loss. All our senses look for a scapegoat. We want to give someone credit for our misery. All we see is God's sovereignty . . . we feel He could have intervened if He had

wanted to. We want pat answers and in the midst of groping for those answers, we often jump to erroneous conclu-
sions.

*Error #1. God used miscarriage and/or stillbirth to punish us
for our sins.* Earlier I shared with you the story of Sharon. She
was struggling with guilt over having had an abortion, and
wondered if God was punishing her through her miscarriage. Many people have the same misconception.

Some people use Old Testament scripture verses to
equate a miscarriage to God's punishment and a successful
pregnancy to God's blessing. Exodus 23:25, 26 is often used.
"Worship the LORD your God, and his blessing will be on
your food and water. I will take away sickness from among
you, and none will miscarry or be barren in your land. I will
give you a full life span." Hosea 9:14 pronounces judgment
against Israel for their unfaithfulness to God and describes
part of their corporate punishment, "Give them, O LORD
what will you give them? Give them wombs that miscarry
and breasts that are dry."

When dealing with a particular subject in scripture, it is
very important to see the overall scriptural view, rather than
to base a conclusion on one or two verses alone. Here it is
important to remember that in the Old Testament God's
blessing and God's judgment were given to the nation of
Israel corporately. This occurred under the Old Covenant
agreement. If Israel obeyed as a nation, God's blessing was
upon them as a nation. If, as a whole, they sinned and followed other gods, then judgment was made on the entire
nation for that sin. However, God no longer relates to us in
a corporate fashion as He did with Israel. Today, on the basis
of the New Testament covenant, God relates to us as individuals.

It is important to know that since Jesus Christ came and
died on the cross for the sins of all mankind, God does not
inflict punishment for our sins. Our sins have been paid for

already. Christ's death on the cross canceled out our debt for sin (Colossians 2:14). Therefore, if we are a Christian and have accepted Christ's gift to us, miscarriage or stillbirth cannot be viewed as punishment for sin. Romans 8:1 says, "There is now no condemnation for those who are in Christ Jesus." My account with God is settled. Christ paid the price for my sins once and for all. Thus, to say that God sent miscarriage or stillbirth as a punishment for sin is biblically inaccurate. God is a just and fair God. It would be contrary to His nature to make me pay for something that was already paid for by His dearly loved Son.

Error #2: God sent miscarriage or stillbirth to build my character and to make me a stronger Christian. One of the common platitudes offered by those trying to console a grieving couple is, "God has a purpose for all this . . . you'll be a much stronger Christian because of this suffering." These comments assume that God is a God who inflicts miscarriage and stillbirth in order to prepare a person for a greater mission in life. The grieving parent's are to look at their pain as an opportunity to become more mature. They are encouraged to think that God must really know they have stamina since He is putting them through this and He promises that "he will not let you be tempted beyond what you can bear" (1 Corinthians 10:13).

There are a couple of questions I have concerning this viewpoint. If God is in fact the one inflicting miscarriage or stillbirth to cause maturity in my life, how can I go to Him for help? In other words, if He is the source of my pain, how could I go to Him for comfort? I couldn't! Only a sadistic God would impose pain and then say, "Let me nurse your wounds and heal your pain." The belief that God initiates a pregnancy loss as a catalyst for achieving spirituality is a fallacy. It assumes He sometimes operates contrary to His nature. Scripture tells us that God is a GOOD, FAIR, KIND, HEALING, JUST, and LOVING Father. Would a loving earthly father purposely inflict suffering on his child and then say, "Come here, let me comfort you and help you in your sorrow?" The thought is ridiculous. Neither would a loving heavenly Father cause a miscarriage or stillbirth and then say, "Now come to me, I'll heal you and you'll have a great spiritual awakening in your life because of this."

Error #3: The devil killed my baby. Margie made these comments: "The devil really did a number on us this time. First he tried to destroy our marriage, and now our son is born dead. Won't he ever leave us alone? What do we have to do so we aren't harassed by him the rest of our lives?"

Margie's viewpoint is common. She and her husband felt certain at the time of their stillbirth that the devil had been involved in taking their son's life. Margie and David have been Christians for sixteen years and love the Lord. But they have felt for the past few years that "the devil was working overtime in them" and was the cause of many of their marital problems and now their son's death. What does scripture have to say about this viewpoint?

First of all, we need to state that the victory of the Christian life is not equal to feeling good, being prosperous, having success, and being problem-free. As Alexander Solzhenitsyn said, "The meaning of earthly existence is not, as we have grown used to thinking, in prosperity but in the development of the soul."[3] So, on what is the victory of the Christian life based? It is tied to and based on the resurrection of Jesus Christ. The devil was defeated at the cross. Read the following verses:

For he has rescued us from the dominion of darkness [Satan's kingdom power] and brought us into the kingdom of the Son he loves, in whom we have redemption, the forgiveness of sins (Colossians 1:13, 14). [We are no longer under Satan's power.]

He who does what is sinful is of the devil, because the devil has been sinning from the beginning. The reason the Son of God appeared was to destroy the devil's work (1 John 3:8). [Victory was established at the cross.]

Jesus said "... Now is the time for judgment on this world; now the prince of this world [Satan] will be driven out. But I, when I am lifted up from the earth, will draw all men to myself" (John 12:31, 32). [When the victory of Christ's kingdom was established, Satan's was demolished.]

... because the prince of this world now stands condemned (John 16:11).

Since the children have flesh and blood, he too shared in their humanity so that by his death he might destroy him who holds the power of death—that is, the devil, and free those who all their lives were held in slavery by their fear of death (Hebrews 2:14,15). [The cross destroyed not only the power of death, but also the fear of death.]

On the basis of these scriptures, you can rest assured that the devil did not kill your baby or cause your miscarriage or stillbirth. He has no power to do such acts. To attribute your loss to the devil is to give him more credit than he deserves.

IF NEITHER GOD NOR SATAN WERE RESPONSIBLE, WHAT HAPPENED?

I'd like to go back to what my nurse, Sharon, shared with me during the moments following the doctor's announcement that our baby was dead. She said, "We live in a fallen world and sometimes the pain and suffering of that fallen world touches our lives. It doesn't seem fair, I know, but nothing will be totally fair and perfect until we get to heaven."

Since our world is fallen we must learn to expect the innocent to sometimes be the victims of heartache. Miscarriage or stillbirth isn't a sign of sin in your life or a message from God to "shape up your act." It is simply a form of suffering common to the human experience of living in this world. Not everything in life is fair or predictable. Many wrongs are not made right. But there will be a day when a final judgment will be made, and at that time everything will be set straight. Until that time I must accept the fact that I will go through times when my human experience is painful. There will be times when I have questions and no answers. There will be times when heartache will be hard to bear. This is all part of living in a fallen world.

While I accept this fact, I can at the same time have hope for bright tomorrows. I know without a doubt that ". . . in all things God works for the good of those who love him..." (Romans 8:28). Some people may read this verse and interpret it this way: God works pain and joy, good and evil into my life for my good. Thus miscarriage or stillbirth was placed into my life by God in order to accomplish good in my life. I prefer to look at it another way. God did not afflict us with a miscarriage to work a certain "good" or growth into our lives. Neither did the devil cause our baby's death. Rather, our lives were touched by the pain of human experience, and in the process of groping for answers and understanding, growth was produced. God's involvement with us in that growth process gave us hope, strength, tenacity, and comfort. As we came to grips with our anger and depression and guilt, God stepped into our human weakness and lifted us out of the depths of despair. That is how God worked good into our lives during our loss. Jesus said, "I have told you these things, so that in me you may have peace. In this world you will have trouble. But take heart! I have overcome the world" (John 16:33).

God knew we would experience the sting of pain and suffering. With that understanding, He offers the encouraging words that He has "overcome the world." So in the midst of my humanness, He can reach into my life and help me stand on my feet again. He brings peace to my turmoil. He brings order to my chaos. He brings hope to my despair. Truly God is a good God!

Chapter Eighteen

The Gift of Letting Go

A fter we lost our baby there were times when I said to myself, "Pam, you've got to let go and move on with your life." It was easier said than done. Letting go is hard work. It's often very confusing and bewildering. To break away from something we have been bonded to tears apart our emotions. It goes against our natural instincts to break bonds. The parting cannot happen without inward bleeding. The greater the bond, the greater the pain.

Our mind and our emotions feel like they are at war with one another. Our head says: "This is what you need to do for your own good. This is what you need to do for the sake of your family." But our heart says: "NO! It hurts too much. I can't do it."

Usually when our awareness of our loss increases, so does our pain. I heard about a poster that showed a cartoon of a woman with her head and arms squeezing through the wringer of an old wringer washing machine. Her face was full of anguish. The caption read: The truth will set you free, but first it will make you miserable. It's very painful to face the full impact of our losses.

Psychiatric research shows that the way to let go of our pain is to feel it. Some of my favorite sayings are "Feeling is healing," and "Birds fly, fish swim, people feel." Stuffing our feelings or numbing them with some sort of addictive behavior prolongs and intensifies our grief and blocks us from successfully letting go. I remember saying to one of my colleagues after my miscarriage, "I wish there was a pill I could take that would make all these painful feelings go away." And his response was, "I can sure understand that, but then you would just have to deal with your grief later." His point was that when I was feeling, I was making progress.

Letting go demands that we let ourselves feel our pain and ride out the grief. If we chose to deny and stuff our pain, we will end up getting stuck in recovery and never fully heal.

But how can we let go? What can we do to help ourselves let go of the pain? I think the place to start is to give ourselves permission to feel and to carve out times in the day when we can release the emotions in a safe place. I found that safe place in my relationship with God.

My first tendency was to retreat from everyone, including God, or to keep myself excessively busy so I wouldn't have to deal with the pain. It's easy to turn to numbing substitutes such as food, alcohol, drugs, novels, shopping or other things to mask the pain. As humans we seem to run faster when we have lost our way.

During the painful times of life, when I am having to let go of something dear to me, I've found that God is the safest One to run to. He knows me better than I know myself. He is the One who can give me insight into my needs. He gives direction when I am confused, and courage when I'm afraid. In weakness I cry out: "God, I can't stop the hurt. No matter what I do it doesn't end. I need your supernatural help. Give me your perspective. Let my eyes see as You see. Let my ears hear your voice. Show me how I can cooperate with You in healing my heart." Prayers of ventilation have helped release my pain.

When we are grieving our prayers seem to go unnoticed or unanswered. Where is God when we are hurting? Does He even care about how we feel? Philip Yancey, in his classic work, *Where Is God When It Hurts?* gives me perspective when life brings pain my way:

> How did God-in-earth respond to pain. When he met a person in pain, he was deeply moved with compassion (pati and cum, "to suffer with"). Not once did he say, "Endure your hunger! Swallow your grief!" When Jesus' friend Lazarus died, Jesus wept.

> Everytime he was directly asked, he healed the pain....I doubt Jesus' disciples tormented themselves with questions like, "Does God care?" They had visible evidence of His love and concern every day: they simply looked at Jesus' face.

> And when Jesus himself faced suffering, he reacted much like any of us would. He recoiled from it, asking three times if there was any other way. In the gospel accounts of Jesus' last night on earth, I detect a fierce struggle with fear, helplessness, and hope— the same frontiers all of us confront in our suffering. How does God feel about our pain? In reply, God did not give us words or theories on the problem of pain. He gave us Himself. A philosophy may explain difficult things, but has no power to change them.[1]

Jesus does have the power. He has the power to change us from the inside out, to heal the pain that seems to have no limits. But He will always be a gentleman. He will never force us to let go of something to which we are clinging. He will compassionately wait for us to release our grip, to open our hands, and to invite Him to participate in our lives. Once our invitation is extended, we have an eternal guarantee that He be with us no matter what life brings our way. And He promises to help us let go of our pain a little at a time. The precious memories of our baby will always be with us. Indeed they are a gift. But in time the heartache connected to those memories will diminish, and life will become more manageable.

One day we will be able to look back and see how God's hand has been on our lives. Hindsight will reveal the new levels of courage and growth that have come to us. And we will smile over the changes we've made. Things will make more sense. But not until history has run its course will we fully understand how "all things work together for good" (Romans 8:28). So, for now we must choose a life of faith. In Yancey's words, that means believing in advance what will only make sense in reverse.[2]

wo years after the loss of our first child, I delivered a beautiful baby girl. Jessie is now a spunky nine-year-old with enthusiasm and zest for life. Just as John's dad predicted she's our little blond-haired, blue-eyed, bubbly one who loves to sing and dance and play the piano.

Three and one-half years later we thought our family was complete with the addition of our precious son, Benjamin. Ben is now five, full of jokes and jollies, and he loves being daddy's helper. Ben can make friends with just about anyone, including the neighborhood snakes. He's our dark-haired, amiable one whose gentle spirit is always quick to please.

Much to our surprise, three and one-half years following Benjamin's arrival, we found out I was pregnant again. John and I were shocked as conception had occurred in spite of what was supposed to be "fool-proof" birth control. September 7th, six weeks prior to my due date, I delivered another special baby boy, Nathan Charles. Trauma surrounded the delivery as Nathan was born blue and floppy. Several days of intensive care followed, along with a diagnosis of Down Syndrome and congenital heart defects.

Once again life forced us to embrace a new kind of pain. We have been told by parents who have raised children with handicaps that the grief never really goes away. The triggers simply change.

Nathan is now twenty months old and into everything. The holes in his heart healed without the need of surgery, and we have had the joy of seeing him learn to walk and to communicate with help of sign language. He's our blond-haired, blue-eyed, affectionate one who we have nicknamed Sunshine. For the most part our family has stabilized and I've begun to see signs of new life emerging in all of us.

Jessie and Ben have matured in unique ways since Nathan joined our family. They are now highly sensitized to the "underdogs" in social circles and go out of their way to

End Notes

Chapter 3
1. C.S. Lewis, *A Grief Observed* (New York, N.Y.: Bantam Books, 1980), p. 69.

Chapter 4
1. H. Norman Wright, *The Christian Use of Emotional Power* (Old Tappan, N.J.: Fleming H. Revell, 1974), pp. 113-115.

Chapter 5
1. Consultation with Dr. Warner B. Swarner, M.D., Psychiatrist, on the use of anti-depressant medication for those in the midst of the grief process. Portland Adventist Medical Center, Portland, Oregon, June, 1994.

Chapter 6
1. Don Baker and Emery Nester, *Depression: Finding Love and Meaning in Life's Dark Shadow* (Portland, Ore.: Multnomah Press, 1983), p. 184.
2. Paul D. Meier and Frank B. Minerth, *Happiness Is a Choice* (Grand Rapids, Mich.: Baker Book House, 1978), p.121.
3. Baker and Nester, *Depression*, p. 185.

Chapter 7
1. Wendy Bergren, *Mom Is Very Sick—Here's How to Help* (Arcadia, Calif.: Focus on the Family Publications, 1982).

Chapter 8
1. J. Cullberg, "Mental Reactions of Women to Perinatal Death," *Psychosomatic Medicine in Obstetrics and Gynecology,* 3rd International Congress, London: 1971, (S. Karger AG, Basel, 1972), p326.

Chapter 10
1. Lynda Madaras and Jane Patterson, *Womancare: A Gynecology Guide to Your Body* (New York, N.Y.: Avon Books, 1981) p. 636.
2. Paavo Airola, *Every Woman's Book* (Phoenix, Ariz.: Health Plus Publishers, 1979), pp 48-76.

Chapter 11
1. Paul Kirk and Pat Schwerbert, *When Hello Means Good-bye* (Portland, Ore.: University of Oregon Health Sciences Center, 1981), p. 11.

Chapter 12
1. Dr. William Sears, Preparing for the Arrival of a Newborn (Arcadia, Calif.: Focus on the Family Publications, 1983).

Chapter 13
1. Bob Schwartz, *Diets Don't Work* (Galveston, Tex.: Breakthrough Publications, 1982), p.209.
2. This material originally appeared in: Pam Vredevelt, *The Thin Disguise* (Nashville, Tenn.: Thomas Nelson Publishers, 1992), pp. 209, 210, 211, 214-219.

Chapter 14
1. C.H. Folkins, M.M. Gardner, and S. L Lynch, "Psychological Fitness as a Function of Physical Fitness," *Archives of Physical Medicine and Rehabilitation* 53 (1972): pp. 503-508; R.S. Brown, D.E. Raminez and J.M. Taub, "The Prescription of Exercise for Depression," *Physicians' Sports Medicine* (June 1978) pp. 34-35; R.R. Eischens, J. Fans, J.M. Griest, and M.H. Klein, "Running out of Depression," *Physicians' Sports Medicine* (June 1978): pp. 49-56.

Chapter 15
1. Laxmi V. Baxi, M.D. and Harold E. Fox, M.D., *The Columbia University College of Physicians and Surgeons Complete Guide to Pregnancy* (New York, N.Y.: Crown Publishers, 1988), p. 246.
2. Bruce D. Shephard and Carroll A. Shephard, *The Complete Guide to Women's Health* (New York, N.Y.: The Penguin Group, A Plume Book, 1990), p. 362.
3. Baxi and Fox, *Complete Guide to Pregnancy*, p. 246.
4. Charles B. Clayman, ed., *The American Medical Encyclopedia* (New York, N.Y.: Random House, 1989), p. 389.
5. Ann Trustem, "When to Suspect Ectopic Pregnancy," *Registered Nurse Magazine* (August, 1991), pp. 22-25.

6. V. Jacson, "The Fallopian Tubes," *Gynecology, Well-Woman Care*, R. Lichtman and S. Papera, eds., (East Norwalk, Conn.: Appleton and Lange, 1990).

7. K.P. Nederlof and H.W. Lawson, "Ectopic Pregnancy Surveillance, United States, 1970-1987," *Morbidity and Mortality Weekly Report*, 39 (SS-4), (1990), p. 9.

8. Niels Laversen and Steven Whitney, *It's Your Body* (New York, N.Y.: the Putnam Publishing Group, 1993), p. 104.

9. Trustem, *Registered Nurse Magazine*, pp. 23-25.

10. Ibid., pp. 23-25.

11. Dr. Arnold L. Petersen II, M.D., P.C., interview by author, Portland, Oregon, June 1994.

12. Alan F. Guttmacher, M.D., *Pregnancy, Birth, and Family Planning* (New York, N.Y.: New American Library, 1973), p. 147.

13. Baxi and Fox, Complete Guide to Pregnancy, p.

Chapter 16

1. Madaras and Patterson, *Womancare*, p.636.

Chapter 17

1. Mary Hanes, "Miscarriage: Comfort from the Bible," *Virtue Magazine* 5 (May/June 1983), p. 68.

2. C.S. Lewis, *The Last Battle* (New York, N.Y.: Macmillan Publishing Co., Inc., 1970), p. 173.

3. Alexander Solzhenitsyn, Gulag Archipelago II (New York, N.Y.: Harper and Row, 1975), p. 613.

Chapter 18

1. Philip Yancy, *Where is God When It Hurts?* (Mich.: Zondervan Publishers, 1990), pp. 225-226.

2. Philip Yancy, *Disappointment with God* (New York, N.Y.: Harper Collins, 1988), p. 237.

References

Airola, Paavo, *Every Woman's Book*. Phoenix, Ariz.: Helath Plus Publishers, 1979.

Baker, Don, and Nester, Emery. *Depression: Finding Hope and Meaning in Life's Darkest Shadow*. Portland, Ore.: Multnomah Press, 1983.

Bailey, Covert. *Fit or Fat*. Boston: Houghton Mifflin Company, 1978.

Bergren, Wendy. *Mom Is Very Sick—Here's How to Help*. Arcadia, Calif.: Focus on the Family Publications, 1982.

Borg, Susan, and Lasker, Judith. *When Pregnancy Fails*. Boston: Beacon Press, 1981.

Carr, D.H. "Chromosome Anomalies as a Cause of Spontaneous Abortion." *American Journal of Obstetrics and Gynecology*. 97 (1967): 283.

Corney, Robert, and Horton, Frederick. "Pathological Grief Following Spontaneous Abortion." *American Journal of Psychiatry* 131, no. 7 (July 1974): 825-827.

Crout, Teresa Kochmar. "Caring for the Mother of a Stillborn Baby." *Nursing 80* 10, no. 4 (April 1980): 70-73.

Curtis, Helena, and Bamer, N. Sue. *Invitation to Biology*. New York: Worth Publishers, 1977.

Dobson, James. *Emotions: Can You Trust Them?* Ventura, Calif.: Regal Books, 1980.

Finch, Dr. Thomas. Cascade Chiropractic Center, Gresham, Oregon. Interview, July 1983.

Jackson, Karlene. "Overcoming the Trauma of Miscarriage." *Virtue Magazine*, May/June, 1983.

Kaplan, Helen. *The New Sex Therapy: Active Treatment of Sexual Dysfunctions*. New York: Brenner-Mazel, 1974.

Kirk, Paul, and Schweibert, Pat. *When Hello Means Goodbye*. Portland, Ore.: University of Oregon Health Sciences Center, 1981.

Kübler-Ross, Elisabeth. *On Death and Dying*. New York: Macmillan Publishing Co., Inc., 1969.

Lewis, C.S. *A Grief Observed*. New York: Bantam Books, 1980.

Madaras, Lynda, and Patterson, Jane. *Womancare: A Gynecological Guide to Your Body*. New York: Avon Books, 1981.

Meier, Paul D., and Minirth, Frank B. *Happiness Is a Choice: Overcoming Depression.* Grand Rapids, Mich.: Baker Book House, 1978.

Pizer, Hank, and O'Brien Palinski, Christini. *Coping with a Miscarriage.* New York: New American Library, 1981.

Sciaria, John J.; Speidel, J. Joseph; and Zantuchini, Gerald I. *Pregnancy Termination: Procedures, Safety, and New Developments.* Hagerstown: Harper & Row Publishers, 1978.

Sears, William. *Preparing for the Arrival of a Newborn.* Arcadia, Calif.: Focus on the Family Publication, 1983.

Seibel, Machelle, and Graves, William L. "The Psychological Implications of Spontaneous Abortions." *The Journal of Reproductive Medicine* 25, no. 4 (October 1980): 161-195.

Tizard, A. "Mourning Made Easier If Parents Can View Body of Neonate." *Obstetrics and Gynecology News* 11, no. 21 (1976): 35.

U.S. Department of Health, Education, and Welfare. *Prevention of Embryonic, Fetal, and Perinatal Disease,* by Robert L. Brent and Maureen I. Harris. DHEW Publication No. (NIH) 76-853. Washington, D.C.: Government Printing Office, 1976.

Wright, Norman. *The Christian Use of Emotional Power.* Old Tappan, New Jersey: Fleming H. Revell, 1974.

Yates, Susan A. "Stillbirth—What a Staff Can Do." *American Journal of Nursing* 72 (September 1972): 1592-1594.